THE ROAD TO BEAVER PARK

Sunshine Peak, San Juan Mountains, Colorado

THE ROAD TO BEAVER PARK

Painting, Perception, and Pilgrimage

By Janice E. Kirk

Janice E Kirk

Ps 27: 4

RESOURCE *Publications* · Eugene, Oregon

THE ROAD TO BEAVER PARK
Painting, Perception, and Pilgrimage

Resource Publications
An Imprint of Wipf and Stock Publishers
199 W. 8th Ave., Suite 3
Eugene, OR 97401

www.wipfandstock.com

PAPERBACK ISBN 13: 978-1-4982-2969-2
HARDCOVER ISBN 13: 978-1-4982-2971-5

Manufactured in the U.S.A.   04/05/2016

All Bible quotations are used by permission, all rights reserved.

Bible texts credited to NIV are taken from The Holy Bible, New International Version, Copyright © 1973, 1978, 1984, International Bible Society, Zondervan Bible Publishers.

Bible texts credited to NLT are taken from the Holy Bible, New Living Translation, copyright © 1996, 2004, 2007 by Tyndale House Foundation. Used by permission of Tyndale House Publishers, Inc., Carol Stream, Illinois 60188. All rights reserved.

Bible texts credited to The Message are taken from The Message. Copyright © 1993, 1994, 1995, 1996, 2000, 2001, 2002. Used by permission NavPress Publishing Group.

Bible texts credited to Moffatt are taken from taken from The Bible, A New Translation. Copyright © 1922,1924, 1925, 1926, 1935, Harper and & Row Publishers. Copyright ©1950, 1952, 1953, 1954. James A. R. Moffatt.

Grateful acknowledgment is made for permission to reprint excerpts from "God's Grandeur" and "The Starlight Night" previously published in Gerard Manley Hopkins, Gerard Manley Hopkins: The Major Works, edited by Catherine Phillips (New York: Oxford University Press, 2009), 128. Reprinted by permission of Oxford University Press on behalf of Society of Jesus.

Map by Mapping Specialists, Ltd.

For Elizabeth and Matthew,
Julia and Jonathan

[It's] not just the spectacular scenery,
the waterfalls and big trees and wildlife ...
It is also about who we see these sacred places with,
whose hand we are holding.

—KEN BURNS, *THE NATIONAL PARKS: AMERICA'S BEST IDEA*

Contents

Illustrations

Preface

My art file overflows with sketches, color studies, and unframed watercolor paintings. Held in reserve because they mean so much, the images record the year that changed everything for me. Over time, each sketch and every painting has become a treasured link to the wonder of a light–filled landscape or portrays detail that suggests the inscape of a solitary flower, tree, river, or dune. The images tell only half the story, however, and in this book, I have recorded the rest.

We stepped away from a fast-paced life one year, went on Sabbatical leave and explored the Greater Southwest. Sketching and painting in the field honed my observation skills and inspired my work. I gained a broadened scope of how nature is put together, literally expanding my horizons. The wholeness of creation, the unity to be found there, became for me a witness to the Source of Creation. It brought me back to Christian faith.

In addition to reviewing my own artwork, research for the book included scanning family journals, Don's photos, Amy's colorful calendars, and visiting National Park Service and other web sites to refresh views and bring information up to date. The best part was sitting with family and asking, "Do you remember when we camped on the San Miguel, on Lehman Creek, or the day we went to the Playa?" Fond memories came flooding back.

We were never the same after that year. Living outdoors generated a familiarity and comfort with nature that all four of us carry to this day. I can still see the overlapping patchwork of plant communities that blanket the West, our life support systems. At times I relive that journey in my mind, and the topography of a huge swath of land once again unfurls, from the northern California Coast, eastward across the Cascades to the ancient lakebeds of the Great Basin, into the rugged reefs and monuments of Mesa and Canyon Country, to the backbone of the North American continent—the

Rocky Mountains, a dramatic contrast to the Colorado prairie—and from there back to Death Valley and Sonoran Desert lands. This grand sweep of earth holds tales to tell and lessons for the alert seeker of outdoor truth who is ready to pay heed, to learn, and who is willing to become a contributing member of our vital life-communities.

I hope my story will encourage readers like you to step outdoors and "take another look." I hope you discover the wonders of the natural world, gain a new perspective, and come to cherish the earth. May the journey bring joy. May it bring peace. May it lead to the Source of Life.

Acknowledgments

Thanks to family for jogging my memory. Thanks especially to Don and Amy, who kept journals. Don's entries covered the first part of the trip from July to November. Unfortunately, his second journal was lost somewhere along the way. Amy wrote her diary during the second half of the trip, and her colorful calendars recorded our itinerary each day. Lots of family photos kept the details accurate, but I have edited journal entries freely. Any inconsistencies are mine alone. Thanks also to the National Park Service and America's state parks. Their active websites not only offer maps, but also animal and plant lists. Their information refreshed facts about geography and geology. If I had questions, the staff obligingly replied to emails and helped to clear up important details.

Thanks to those who were kind enough to critique my early drafts. I appreciate your eagle eyes and helpful comments. At the risk of leaving someone out—please forgive me—I am grateful to Allan Hansen, Brian Larsen, Daun Weiss, Edy Harrington, Judy Gama Strausser, Marilyn Livingston, Ned Livingston, Maxine Cambra, Nancy Milton, Pat Underwood, Robert Milton, Tammy Douse, Tom Wolph, and Ryan Belong. My especial thanks to Caroline Kirk, Maggi Milton, and to my husband, Don Kirk, who read the manuscript more than once and gave thoughtful and unflinchingly honest critiques.

I also wish to acknowledge my debt to art instructors Bert Oldham and Elizabeth Burnham. Even though it has been many years since my classes at Shasta Community College in Redding, California, their artistic teachings still echo in my ear. My thanks also to Pastor Bill Feeser of Saint James Lutheran Church in Redding, whose encouragement and spiritual insights have expanded my understanding of the joyful Christian Way.

Readers will appreciate the camping freedom we had in 1976–1977, but times have changed. Today more campers are enjoying the outdoors.

Too many can overwhelm beautiful places, ruin campsites, and destroy local habitats. Forty years have passed since our trip. In most of the places I mention, open camping has changed to recreational day use only, or the sites have become regulated campgrounds. Our thanks to the U.S. Forest Service, Bureau of Land Management, State Parks, and the National Park Service for guarding the beautiful and sacred places of the earth and for constantly improving their campgrounds.

PROLOGUE

Sabbatical 1976–1977
A Time Apart

WE TOOK NATE, AGE eleven, and Amy, age nine, out of school along with borrowed math, social studies, and spelling books. We rented the house to friends and arranged to have our mail forwarded. We packed the trailer and camper truck with provisions, camping equipment, fishing gear, and even my featherweight sewing machine. Don installed a CB radio as a safety factor and purchased Walkie-Talkies. The children stored their pup tent, sleeping bags, and assorted books and treasures in the camper benches. Don packed camera gear, snake hook, fly rod, and tackle box. He bought a rock hammer for each of us, and we declared ourselves rock hounds. His study project would take us to the Rocky Mountains in the fall and the Sonoran Desert in the spring. This would be a firsthand look at wild edible plants and their plant communities, studies that were central to his graduate work. Don packed every available natural history field guide and ready-reference in the book box. That's when I determined I needed a project too: I would use the time to finally master watercolor painting.

I gathered my student painting equipment into my old wooden paint-box. I purchased a dozen nine-by-twelve-inch sketchbooks, extra tubes of watercolor paint, and a Boy Scout backpack with square corners that was just the right size. I pre-cut good watercolor paper to store under bunk cushions along with a large, sturdy board for support. I also packed drawing pencils, erasers, drafting pens, and India ink in a metal tackle box.

That year I painted *en plein air*, which meant I was at the mercy of wind and sun, gnats, mosquitoes, and deer flies, disturbed by passers-by and visiting dogs. I was too warm or too cold by turns. I grew alert to crawling ticks and free-range cattle. Yet that year I carried my art pack and folding stool into some of the most incredible landscapes on the planet: the canyons, deserts, mountains, and river valleys of the western United States. Awed, amazed, and humbled by what we found there, I sketched with pen and pencil and worked with watercolor paints. I looked, walked, listened, sniffed, and absorbed the changes in temperature and the shift of air currents. I felt the miracle of rain, saw the contrast of light and shade, and observed the myriad forms of leaf and twig and branching vine, insects, small mammals, fish, and fowl. To this day, my mind overflows with those images of abundant life.

For all of us, this was no intellectual exercise. This was a journey of the heart. We grew to love the way the great outdoors is put together. Daily we came to know it better and to understand what makes it work. Each day held something different: field study, fishing trip, sketching trip, photo shoot, rock hunt, picnic, travel adventure, wildflower quest, or discovery hike. After fourteen months, we returned home with field study completed and watercolors in hand. Yet our Sabbatical study trip surprised me with more than I ever anticipated or planned. Somewhere along the way, our journey of respite and renewal turned into pilgrimage.

The most important thing is the awakening.
That joy of awakening and discovery is what it's like to be a child.[1]

---

1. Paul Gorman, qtd. in Louv, *Last Child in the Woods*, 296.

PART I

Point out the road I must travel;
I'm all ears, all eyes before you.

—Ps 143:8b The Message

Rocky Point, Patrick's Point State Park, Northern California Coast

1

The Pacific Coast
Trial Run, April 1976

Tide splash, transition, and other time

Look for the edges between habitats: where the trees stop and a field begins;
where rocks and earth meet water. Life is always at the edges.[1]

"Watch out for sneaker waves," Don hollers. "Keep one eye on the sea!"
Nate and Amy dash toward the ocean. "Cold water will keep them from
going out too far," he adds, "and the water is shallow for a long way out."
We turn away from the beach. I shoulder my art pack and follow Don into
the dunes.

Walking with a naturalist is hardly heart-pumping exercise. We amble
along, look, touch, sniff crushed leaves, and listen to the surf. We note locations and area conditions. Don points out the lay of the land. Natural
drainage troughs serve to channel runoff. Signs of erosion mark the dunes.
Dune succession is easy to see on this beach, from flat sand to foredunes,
back dunes, and coastal land.

The dunes have their own ecosystem. The early springtime wildflowers beg identification. Don pulls out the wildflower guide to check names:

---

1. Ibid., 172.

beach pea, dune tansy, bush lupine. White-crowned sparrows flit through the chaparral broom. We follow deer tracks in the mud where a small creek meanders to the sea. I stop to sketch dune grasses, lines of slender stalks bending with the wind.

We top the rise of a major dune and gaze out to sea. The flat beach extends north and fades into fog near the headland.

"Are we really going to do this for a whole year?" I ask.

Don grins at me. It's unbelievable! Don has been granted a sabbatical leave. Officially it's field study in the Rockies and the Southwest. For once we will have the freedom to explore during fall and springtime, the very months that are impossible on a school schedule. I am brimming with questions and plans.

My tour leader plunges down the sandy slope to the beach. I follow, a shoe-filling endeavor. The beach is partly land, partly water, and the balance shifts back and forth. The sand looks barren but is home to a mixture of plants and animals both aquatic and terrestrial. Don calls this a transition zone, technically an ecotone, since it is rich with life from both land and sea. "Transition zone" rings in my ear. An appropriate term to describe not only the beach, but also us at this moment in our lives. A year apart from our normal routines and home habitat will change us all.

We separate. Don wanders over to where the children dig near the water. I plunk down beside a low mound in the sand. I empty sand out of my shoes and admire the hardy plant—sand verbena—that clings tenaciously to the shifting landscape. The wind peppers me with tiny grains, but I open my sketchbook and draw the yellow blooms. I move to the other side of the mound and find a warm spot out of the wind. I sink back against a driftwood log. My mind spins. Will the tent trailer be adequate? We need warmer clothes and blankets. Will the children keep up with their studies? What about mail delivery? And will the house be OK? Will togetherness become a burden? How am I going to spend my time? I have the answer to that. I will review my art lessons, hone my drawing and painting skills, and perhaps, at long last, I will learn to paint watercolors. I will have time to practice, practice, practice.

My first day *en plein air* is less than productive. My senses are overwhelmed. The warmth of the sun, soft sand, the space of sea and sky before me—I want nothing more than to sit and absorb it all. This sandy earth feels more solid than I remember. Every move I make hollows out even more sand, shaping a bowl to hold me in place. I squint in the bright light, the better to see down the beach to the waterline. That flat playground is the edge of the landmass that rises out of the sea. I draw with my eyes the long undulating lines of surf and beach that disappear into the distance. The view expands into space—infinite space and light—everywhere light in the overarching sky. My art professor would point out that I'm looking at the most basic art components: mass, space, and light.

At times like this, why is it I feel so much a part of the earth? What draws me to the vastness of space? Why do I seek the light?

A wind gust scatters sand over me and ends my reverie. I put my sketchbook away. I can't paint today. The wind will blow sand into my watercolor pans and ruin the colors. I shoulder my pack and run to catch up with my family.

We walk the waterline and sidestep incoming surges that swirl over the sand. Bits of seaweed and aquatic grasses float on the tide and drape themselves gracefully on the beach. I stoop to pick up a perfect snail shell, a tiny marvel of functional housing. Small pieces of sculpted driftwood lay half buried in the sand, along with scraps of bright orange-and-white crab shells. I can't resist reaching for occasional stones that glisten in the receding water. Smooth and round, the white pebbles lay in my hand like small moons.

The children dance around us, playing tag with the waves. They spot the first sand dollar shell and race back to show us. Off come their shoes, and splashing begins in earnest. I kick off my sneakers and wade into the shock of cold water. Waves rush in. I am knee-deep. I hold my breath as the tide pulls away again, swirling sand around my feet. Laughing, we splash back toward shore, our feet blue from the cold. The next wave follows right behind us, and we run to rescue our shoes.

On this day of sun and sand and splashing tide, we first sense "other" time—something apart. Our odyssey will not be governed by clocks or calendars, just seasons and cycles, day and night, patterns of existence that break up time, define it, give it a point of reference. I watch the waves come in. The rhythmic succession flows shoreward. With my artist's eye, I try to memorize the curving path of tidewaters, the ripples on the surface. Those lines on paper will take on their own rhythm. The tide swirls higher, and we scramble even farther back on the sand to put on our shoes. Our space-time dimension has come right down to practical matters: it's lunchtime.

We enjoy two more days before the rains begin. We hike the Rim Trail, which leads into deep forests of spruce and fir. I sketch ferns with their own rhythmic leaf patterns and spirals of emerging new fronds. When Don and the children take the long trail down to the rocks, I sit on an overlook bench and try with little success to paint the ocean view, with its shoreline curving into the distance. My painting is too watery, too pale. Later we all stand at the rail and hand around binoculars, looking for the unmistakable spout of water that signals a whale.

Each evening we hike down to the rocks and wait for sunset colors. We climb onto gigantic boulders and sit as close to the crashing waves as we dare, just out of the waterline. We identify brown pelicans that fly close to us in follow-the-leader formation. They rise and dip like trained dancers. Western gulls idle along the tide line, pecking at piles of seaweed. An enormous wave crashes right in front of us, spraying our rock as we scramble. I jump back from the front slab to the next one. Deep in the crevice between the massive sedimentary boulders, the tidewater swirls around, bringing garbage with it. A plastic jug and other debris float onto a gravel bar and stay there. How out of place it looks, how wrong. I turn away.

The low sun disappears behind a fog bank on the horizon. Colors soften somewhat to an orange-violet, but the fog veils any dramatic drop into the ocean. My painterly eye records the monochromatic color scheme. Why does it seem so right? Everything belongs here except the garbage.

We sit a few moments longer in the twilight that separates daylight from the darkness of the coming night. I study the series of gray tones that now cloak the rhythm of the sea. What a lesson in values! Only a master painter could manage so many gradations of gray without losing the scene.

The children lead the way up the steep trail by the fading light. It is time for campfire stories, hot cocoa, and early-to-bed. Tomorrow we will hike the redwood grove a few miles north of camp.

A wind comes up in the night. It sighs through the trees and scatters fog drip that has collected on needles and branches. The huge drops of water resound on the roof of the tent trailer. By morning, the rain has begun in earnest—a soft, steady, soaking drizzle. We scrap plans for our redwood hike. We play games and read the books we brought. Later we drive to the grocery store to buy seafood and get a weather forecast. The coastline is socked in; clouds and rain will continue for several days.

Nate has caught a cold, and we can't keep warm enough in the tent trailer. At night when I climb into bed, the bedding is damp where the outer edge of the mattress meets the tent. By morning, the dampness has crept inward. We have no good way to dry it out. The four of us huddle inside the trailer discussing our options. Clearly, this arrangement will not do for prolonged bad weather. We need a rig that can handle minor illness, storms, wind, and desert heat. We pack up and head home. The redwoods will have to wait.

[God] alone stretches out the heavens and treads on the waves of the sea . . . When he passes me, I cannot see him; when he goes by, I cannot perceive him.

—JOB 9:8, 11, NIV

Piñon Pine Cone, Nevada

2

The Great Basin, Nevada

Eagle Lake and Bob Scott Campground

Sagebrush country, a horned toad, and desert art

"Wait, Mom!" Nate shouts just as I am shutting the house door. "The bug net!" He dives past me at the last minute to find that basic piece of equipment. I'm glad he thought of it now. Don is already in the driver's seat, but the rest of us—Amy, teenage cousin Tevis, and me—pace beside the truck and trailer. I rack my brain for anything else we might be forgetting as I dig into my purse for dark glasses.

Our neighbor shouts from the fence, "God bless you! Have a great time!"

I wave back and smile. Little do I realize how prophetic her farewell will prove to be. At this moment, however, I doubt that God has anything to do with this trip. We have taken to heart the old Scout motto: "Be prepared." Well, we will be once the bug net is found.

Nate comes back panting. "It was under my bed," he says.

Don asks, "Do we have the snake hook?"

The answer is affirmative, so we all climb in and Don gears up for the long ride ahead. It's July of 1976, and we are finally on our way. Our homemade camper sits like a little cabin on the four-wheel-drive pickup truck. The new twenty-foot Prowler travel trailer follows along behind. We are going to love it; it's self-contained with a bathroom and even a shower, and it will be our protection against bad weather and travel conditions. Not to be forgotten, Don and the boys have loaded the rowboat upside-down onto the top of the trailer. They dream of lake-fishing in the Rockies.

Our road leads out of the valley and rises into the Northern California foothills. The United States of America is two hundred years old this month—land of the free, home of the brave. We venture forth.

> DON: *Already delayed one day because of car trouble, so I stop to check things on way to Lassen. Discover two of three boat straps have come loose. If I hadn't tied the boat on at the rear with rope at the last minute, we would have lost our boat. We stop at Bogard Ranger Station for lunch. Temperature warm. Drive on to Eagle Lake. Hot. Park in camp next to someone else from home.*
>
> *Eagle Lake sits in an ancient crater mostly forested with ponderosa pine, some incense cedar, and open areas of sage. Lake is warm, water level quite low. Western grebes common. Two grebes in courtship ritual dive to the shallow bottom; each picks up a large strand of algae in its beak. They surface and present the algae symbolically to each other almost neck-to-neck, then swim side-by-side, peering this way and that, drop the algae, and make up-and-down motions with their necks, bending them into sharp shepherd's crooks. Looks painful, but to the birds it's a necessary preliminary to breeding.*
>
> *Osprey fly about one hundred feet overhead. Also in camp: yellow pine chipmunks, gray squirrels, golden-mantled ground squirrels, Steller's jays, deer, even cattle. Robins all about. A young one hops after an adult bird, chirping mightily, and finally pecks at the ground. All it gets is a beak full of pine needles, but it will soon learn.*

The next day, we break camp early, too excited to sleep. The morning drive leads down out of the Cascades into western Nevada sagebrush country. We turn east at Reno, and the Great Basin Desert unfolds—undulating foothills, alkali lakebeds, meadows dotted with cattle, dry washes, and rocky canyons. Wide valley floors give rise to mountain ranges colored by minerals, sparsely vegetated at their lower altitudes, and topped by timbered upper slopes.

Sand Mountain comes into view. An artist's delight, the sculptured white dune stands out against dark blue mountains in a windswept gallery of pure form. Dunes are unexpected in this part of the desert, and we stop to photograph. The white sand is made up of quartz particles ground from Sierra granite by ancient glaciers. Over the centuries it washed down to the

Walker River Delta. Picked up by winds that swept across the desert, the sand was deposited over thirty miles to the northeast at the foot of these mountains. The white dunes have built up to about six hundred feet high. With our binoculars we can see a dune buggy nearing the top and a family of hikers.

Don and Tevis set up their cameras. Nate and Amy scout around in the sage. Amy stalks a small butterfly that flutters from bush to bush, just out of reach. It looks like a Sand Mountain Blue butterfly, unique to this area. Nate spots a horned toad partially submerged in the sand and catches it. Not a toad at all but a lizard, it is fairly docile and submits to being handled. Its back is covered with red-and-gray spines that look exactly like miniature mountain ranges, a living topography of perfect protective colors. The children carefully examine the horned lizard. I walk a short distance away to listen for singing dunes. Shifting sand can produce a soft rustling sound, even an eerie boom at times. I listen intently, but today the desert only whispers, a soft stirring in the sage, not singing. I'll have to come back. We load up again. Nate reluctantly lets the lizard go. It belongs here, not in captivity.

The next sagebrush valley opens wide. Don points out ancient water-marks on the hills that ring the basin: old lake levels long forgotten. The land assaults my senses as we drive. Mountains rise and fall, stretching away into the distance with a geologic rhythm. This is basin-and-range topography—a series of north-south mountain ranges that spread across Nevada. To me, they look like stupendous waves on a sagebrush ocean.

We drive halfway across the state, negotiating canyons before we climb yet another mountain pass. The highway follows the Pony Express route of the late 1860s for some distance. We stop to see the ruins of crumbling stone walls where the way station served riders along the old east-west track. Don identifies rabbitbrush and other plants. We hunt for the spring but find no sign of a water source. They must have had a good water supply nearby. We keep glancing at the horizon, and I half expect a lone rider to appear and sweep past us in a cloud of dust. History comes alive in the imagination.

DON: *Bright sunshine today. Head for Bob Scott campground east of Austin, Nevada. Arrive about 3:00 p.m. and set up travel trailer. The boys and I go four-wheeling to the south up Austin Mountain. Elevation here is about 7500 feet. Beautiful aspen groves grow high on the mountainside, with no other trees around. Lower down are forests of piñon pine.*

In the evening at the camp table, we read parts of *Roughing It*, Mark Twain's story of traveling by stagecoach on a different route across this desert. That was in the days of the silver and gold strike in Virginia City, Nevada. The stagecoach was filled with mailbags, which required that Twain and his brother lie on top of the pile. As the stage traversed this rough, untamed territory, the brothers bounced and slid around, fending off Twain's unabridged dictionary, which "avalanched" loose as the coach shifted, threatening damage to life and limb. We laugh, but next morning we make sure everything is tied down before we start out.

> DON: *Late in the night, a hippie couple pulls in across from us and camps. They drive an old 1953 Dodge. Early morning around 6:00, they try to start up and can't, so they find somebody up who has jumper cables. All the noise, confusion, and car exhaust makes it impossible to sleep, so we get up too. We walk up to the prospect hole where last evening the kids found garnet-like quartz just lying on the ground. Turns out to be a cinnabar prospect hole, the quartz stained with iron. Take off about 9:30 from Bob Scott and head to Lehman Caves, seventy-five miles past Ely. Heavy headwind again.*

Every turn of the road brings new images. In the desert sunlight, I'm especially struck by strong contrasts of dark junipers against low brush. Shadowed cliff faces oppose rounded hill shapes. A lone cottonwood casts dramatic shadows, the darkest element for miles. My art lessons for the day are in the vivid contrasts and rhythmic placement of earth forms.

During lunch break, I pull out my watercolors and try to paint the fleeting pictures. Watery blobs are all I can make of the hill shapes. It looks like I have never had a lesson in my life, but as a matter of fact, I have done lots of drawing, including a year spent sketching wild edible plants. I have taken three classes in watercolor, but somehow this is different. Lacking the control of classroom or home studio, I am all thumbs with my travel equipment, and the wind is blowing my paper. I need some large clips or a rubber band. Lessons are all very well, but I know at some point every serious artist has to figure out how to do it their way, find their own images, learn what works for them, and develop a personal style.

I sigh and prop my sketchpad against my art pack to dry. My visual memory doesn't translate to paper yet. Not only is my technique poor—too much water in the brush—I am overwhelmed by the variety of landscapes and forms I see along the road. Something tugs at my memory; I feel like

I have been here before. Aren't these the same art elements I identified at the coast?

It's the big three: *Mass*—the desert showcases earth forms so varied and at times so enormous that I gain a new sense of reality. From boulders by the side of the road to whole mountain ranges that rise dignified and implacable, the contours unfurl as the road winds through them. *Light*—the abiding light of the sun casts brilliance and shadow in varying degrees from light to dark as it dominates the daytime sky. It illuminates the wonders of the earth down to the smallest detail. *Space*—the hollows of valley and canyon depths are filled with space that extends in all directions, boundless. It fills the immense bowl of the sky from horizon to horizon and beyond.

> DON: *Driving across the Great Basin Desert, we see a steady progression from arid to moist conditions. There's more diversity in the plant cover. Every mountain range appears wetter and higher, with increasingly lush plant and animal communities. The Snake Range is the highest. That's where we're going. All this space expands the mind. We see bigger, think bigger, breathe bigger.*

The children clear the picnic table, and we travel on. I'm beginning to agree with Bernard de Fontenelle (1657–1757), the French mathematician and philosopher who said, "I always think of nature as a great spectacle, somewhat resembling the opera."[1] Scene after scene rolls by. My road-riding viewpoint is changing. I no longer think in terms of mileposts, road conditions, camp comforts, or time schedules. Mentally, I shift into drawing mode. We round another curve, and each rock, bush, tree, and creek bed takes on a particular identity—an actuality. My artistic instincts prod me to render each particular form in literal detail. I want to capture the descriptive line, shape, gesture, and character that give individuality. Don, my resident naturalist, itches to study it all, to accurately describe true-to-life behavior, character, role, status, position, capacity, and especially relationships. It's clear that he and I bear a kindred spirit that is at once curious and creative. Artist and scientist both begin with hands-on, ground-level observation. To skip this step of learning is to miss basic information.

Don gears down for the slow climb up the last mountain pass of the day. Slow speed is all the better for me to see what's alongside the road. From short grasses to mountainside terrain, the scenic wonders roll past. We travel in a monumental work of art.

1. De Fontenelle, *Lapham's Quarterly*, 264.

❧

Give me your lantern and compass, give me a map, So I can find my way.

—Ps 43:3, THE MESSAGE

Lehman Creek, Snake Range, Eastern Nevada

3

The Great Basin, Nevada

Snake Range and Lehman Creek.

Sky island, star watch, and fishing is good

DON: *Cool cloudy day. West of Ely, we get some real rain and, in the distance, a beautiful desert lightning and thunderstorm. Arrive at Lehman Caves about 4:00 p.m. Much wetter than last year—lots of rosehips and still green. Some mahonia nearby, very few wildflowers, but then it is past the season for them. Aspen look better than in the past, with larger, greener leaves and less leaf-miner damage. Good drinking water here.*

The turnoff leads uphill out of the ocean of sage and shrubs that covers Snake Valley. A long, slow climb onto the flanks of the Snake Range brings us up into what will one day become Great Basin National Park. We get lucky—one campsite is still open alongside Lehman Creek. Lush growths of willow, wild roses, and aspen welcome us with greenery and shade. It's a relief to be off the road and out of the sun. First order of the day is off with the shoes and a splash in the creek. Amy and I race to see who can get to the water first. The sparkling stream is fresh from snowfields high on Wheeler Peak. It's cold, cold, cold, so I don't wade very long. I dry off and go back to the picnic table to pull out brushes and paints. After three days of scanning the desert panorama, I have finally begun to sort out visual detail. My eye is more selective. Desert colors emerge from brilliant light. Fine lines and precise shapes materialize from rocks and cliffs. My visual memory is better, but I still use too much water on the brush.

Next morning, we tag along with our naturalist to learn the names of plants and animals and why they live here. Don shows us how to use pocket field guides. We identify the yellow monkey flower that drapes the creek bank. Next we find yarrow, larkspur, Indian paintbrush, and a straggly scarlet gilia. The handsome shrub that landscapes our neighbor's campsite is cliffrose—the small creamy blossoms form a pleasing contrast against the dark green waxy leaves. As we get farther from the creek, we find clumps of prickly pear cactus lurking in the dry grass; the yellow flowers look fragile in the blazing sun. Clumps of yellow buckwheat dot the hillside. Down along the road, a Rocky Mountain bee plant stands forth in full display, its rosy blossoms abuzz with a great many bees. Farther on, we find milkweed and chicory.

Don points out major plant communities: Valley sagebrush grows uninterruptedly from basin to foothills and threads into the mountain forest. Rabbitbrush follows the sage and is just beginning to show yellow buds for the late summer and fall bloom. Riparian plants, the water-loving plants that thrive along the creek banks, include roses, wildflowers, and the quaking aspen that shiver in the breeze. The aspen spread uphill into the next major plant community: the belt of ponderosa pine that dominates the upper slopes all the way to timberline. Lower down it's drier, and the forest shifts into a mix of juniper and piñon pine that mingles with mountain mahogany. Some piñons bear green cones. Each day, we watch the squirrels test for ripe, sweet piñon nuts, but the cones are not yet ready for harvest.

Wildlife thrives around us. A chipmunk family lives near our camp table, which is no doubt a steady food supply for the little bandits. Birds and deer wander through camp. Interwoven lives of plants and animals make this community what it is. It's good to know our neighbors; it makes us feel at home.

Tevis and Nate go fishing. Amy plays in the creek while I sketch. My drawing skills are put to good use recording the abundant life here. I have learned the names, and now I will memorize the faces.

DON: *Oil my boots, then photograph the creeping mahonia, including aphids. Large numbers of creeping mahonia have ripening berries. When ripe, the berries are light blue with a whitish bloom. Many sport dried berries and leaves already turned a beautiful scarlet. All the plant's energy seems to be going toward maturing the berries. The berries are quite sour, but Indian people made great use of them, as did pioneers. These mahonia seem to prefer partial shade, for they are found beneath juniper, piñon, aspen, and mountain mahogany.*

In the evening, Nate and Tevis build a small campfire. We celebrate with roasted marshmallows and watch as encroaching darkness spreads over the landscape. The encircling shrubs turn into dark silhouettes, and two fireflies lift off from the shrubbery. What are they doing out here in the desert? The book says they don't live west of the Rockies. Amy tries to catch one, but uneven ground and poor light hamper her chase. Stars take over from the fireflies, winking awake in the deepening blue overhead. Slowly, the sky becomes a wonder of scattered brilliance, and stardust lights the Milky Way. Closer to the horizon, large vibrant stars hover just above the treetops. At first we "ooh" and "ah" and point out constellations, then we tell star stories for a while, but little by little we fall silent. No city lights intrude; no moon shines tonight; only the darkest of dark reigns as the backdrop for this wondrous glimpse of the universe.

The campfire smolders to coals. Somewhere across the creek, a lone coyote howls. We strain to hear more. Night knowledge is so dependent on sound. Perception heightens, and we listen, listen, waiting for the darkness to reveal itself. Yet in the quiet I hear no animal movement, no earth sighs. Instead, a new sensation wells up within me—a longing, an ache that surfaces from deep inside. For what? To belong? To know the unknowable? Something beyond?

The fire is dark. Silence deepens, and a comforting blanket of peace spreads through the camp. With it comes a sense of rightness, of wholeness. Long moments pass. We stargaze until the night chill creeps down the canyon. Then one by one we murmur goodnight and head for the warmth of sleeping bags.

I lie in bed and hear the footfall of a deer that browses past the trailer. Stars still guard the night; the creek murmurs a blessing. My yearning returns and with it a new awareness: a listening. At length, the peace of the night enfolds my questing spirit. Aspen leaves whisper a benediction, and I sleep.

DON: *Last night, a mouse ran around the campsite, or at least Amy says so. In fact, she claims it ran right over her sleeping bag. She was sleeping outside on the ground, so she moved in to the trailer. Tev and Nate slept out on the ground too. They stayed outside. This day has dawned bright and warm with a few wispy clouds.*

In the morning, the creek water runs about a foot lower. Overnight, the cold temperatures high on Wheeler Peak have slowed the thaw of snowbanks and lessened the runoff. I splash my face with creek water and tingling from the cold, I set out for a wakeup walk. I surprise three deer in the meadow just below the campground. Golden-mantled ground squirrels scamper across the road in front of me. Close to the creek, a meadowlark bursts into song with a throaty, cheerful call. Early light puts a shine on meadow grasses and the willows by the creek. The whole world seems full of light. With the mountain at my back, I can see for miles from the creek down the slope of sagebrush to the valley floor. The distant Utah mountain range seems close, maybe five miles or so, but I know it is more than thirty miles across the valley. We are on a "sky island," a mountain range completely surrounded by sagebrush and cut off from other mountains.

What a lesson in perspective! Sagebrush and grasses near at hand display bold shapes and strong color. As the slope swoops down and away from me, the shapes become smaller and their edges less distinct. Colors pale as the rhythmic lines of the land converge in the distance at the vanishing point where earth and sky meld together. I understand the perspective of converging lines, a beginning lesson for every art student. This view shows more. Clarity, strength of color, and size of objects make a difference in correctly rendering the near and far. Here's the art lesson for my next landscape attempt.

What shaped this land? What processes were at work here? It looks like a giant hand scooped away this glacier-carved canyon and then spread mountain detritus downhill in a wide, fan-shaped slope. Weather and gravity helped lay out the geologic forms; time has softened the rough places into graceful lines and contours.

The high mountains behind me catch most of the moisture from the rainclouds that blow through. The seasonal snowmelt from glaciers and snowbanks feeds two high-altitude lakes and this tumbling stream. I can see Don's hat above the willows as he fishes along the creek. As the life-giving water moves down the slope, the vegetation changes. The lush creek habitat gives way to shrubs and grasses that require less and less water as the land broadens out. Water that seeps underground emerges in odd niches as springs and trickles, the source of life to smaller plant and animal communities.

The valley floor receives little moisture. Despite this limiting factor, the plants have adapted to whatever water is available. Lizards, birds, rodents, small mammals, and large ones inhabit this desert. Life thrives here.

Limitation is a creative principle of art, a working principle, a crafter's principle. When an artist limits the work to a few elements, such as color, media, or subject matter, the scope of the work is narrowed. To include a bit of everything overwhelms the focus and, in this case, resources. Limitation, in turn, sparks creativity—the artist must use more ingenuity to come up with clever variations. This desert valley is alive with adaptive plants and animals. No wonder the living earth is called the creation.

Amy catches up with me just as I round the lower bend of the road. The three deer raise their heads. The two does munch placidly, but the younger deer is nervous and moves away. By the time we complete the loop back to camp, Don, Nate, and Tev are coming up from the creek with fresh-caught trout. Hurray! Trout for breakfast. After that, we plan to go see Lehman Caves.

Where is God my Maker, who gives songs in the night,
who teaches more to us than to the beasts of the earth
and makes us wiser than the birds of the air?

—JOB 35:10–11 NIV

Snake Valley, Eastern Nevada

4

The Great Basin, Utah

The Playa

Fossils alive, a poorwill, and silence

WE PACK A LUNCH and leave word with the ranger in case we don't get back by nightfall. We are heading for a remote area today, and even though we carry extra food, water, and fuel, it is good for someone to know our whereabouts if we should get stranded. We start driving across the valley toward the distant mountain range. On the other side of the mountains lies a playa, an alkaline lakebed that was covered with water just a few thousand years ago. It's strange to think of so much water in this dry desert. Of course, 10,000 years ago, this was not desert. The climate was more like what we have today in the Rocky Mountains or the Sierras of California. Don and I have been to this place before, and we want to show the children.

> DON: *Driving to the playa today, very remote. Nearest gas station is sixty miles away. Jan and I were here in 1961. Hills surrounding the old lakebed show sagebrush, piñon pine, and juniper. Sage in the arid valley is short and stubby. Nothing, absolutely nothing grows on the playa, which is about two miles wide. We head for the east shore—the north end is about four miles away; the south end is out of sight down the distant desert valley.*

We wind down the desert mountain pass, and I glimpse the distant expanse of flat, white land that shimmers in the sun. Alkali white tire tracks lead off the highway across a jumble of hills. I make mental notes as the two tire tracks converge around curves, separate again on the straight stretches, then melt into the distant playa—perspective in action. The tracks lead straight across the lakebed, as level a road as can be found anywhere. In the middle of the white lakebed, a rocky island rises to a height of several hundred feet. Don estimates that a walk around it is probably about a quarter of a mile. Fossils of ancient organisms can be found on the island and in the nearby hills. We cross the hardpacked alkali flat. Not a drop of water exists in this white expanse except at the far end. Don pulls to a stop, not too close to an enormous, milky mud puddle. The children tumble out of the truck to investigate this oddity. I pull out my sketchbook.

> DON: *The playa is smooth and cracked in geometric patterns like dried mud everywhere. We can safely go thirty or forty miles per hour—no rocks, no gullies, no logs. We kick up a white dust cloud and head for the only water hole, which is roughly circular and about thirty yards across. We park a safe distance from it in case of soft mud. This water hole is not just a depression in the lake bottom where water collects; it is a desert spring. Endless wind stirs up alkali mud from the shallow bottom, which makes for muddy, milky water.*

The white alkali is blindingly bright. I move my sketchbook out of direct sun and draw the lake, bordered by hills, which are broken and rough. This is forbidding territory, dry and bleak. The playa stretches out into the distance on one side to a very low horizon, which gives a sense of limitless space. To my left, the rugged hills curve around the old lakebed. Ancient waterlines are still visible along the base of the cliffs.

I draw the skyline along the top ridge and try to capture every bump and rise of the rocks. As I squint, the hills recede in importance, and the lower line of sky takes on its own shape. This reverse focus is what artists call negative space, or the area around an object. "Nothing" has a shape too, just like the "something" that is the object of focus. For the artist, this negative shape is as important as the positive. The "nothing" shape must be in harmonious balance with the rest of the composition. I draw the skyline and find I have rendered the top ridge of the mountains. Same line, the only difference is in my focus.

> DON: *No breeze, but the milky water surface is agitated. Desert shrimp! Thrilled to find them! Sized three inches or so in length;*

horseshoe-shaped carapace covers the back; segmented tail is forked
at the end; and two eyes, like spots in the carapace at the head-end.

I prepare a tray with a few rocks from the island and a bit of
sand. Pour in clear water from one of our water cans. The boys catch
a couple of shrimp, which I photograph in my makeshift field photo
setup. Shrimp in the tray are hyperactive and difficult to calm down.
Eventually manage a photo. These are living fossils, since they have
changed very little in hundreds of millions of years.

When the shout goes up from the puddle explorers, I hurry over to
see what they have found. Small, off-white, primitive creatures that look
like seafood swim in the milky water. They rise to the surface then dive out
of sight. What a mystery! Tev runs back to the truck for the dip net, and he
and Nate scoop a few desert shrimp into Don's pan so we can get a good
look at them. The last time Don and I were here, we saw no sign of life in
that alkali water. The creatures must have been dormant. Are these edible?
This family loves to eat shrimp from the ocean, but I don't think we'll try
these. Where did the first shrimp come from? Were they in the original lake
eons ago? We have more questions than we have answers.

DON: *Drive over to the dry wash at lake's edge to hunt for fossils.*
Show family how to dig into the cliff. We find trilobites and a couple
of fossil sponges that are only a few inches in diameter. We also find
a few fossils of desert shrimp, which resemble the horseshoe crabs of
today's oceans.

A sense of antiquity goes with us as we drive to the end of the lakebed.
We park near a large dry wash that leads into a fold in the hills. It gradually
narrows to a small canyon. Ever-mindful of rattlesnakes, we walk up the
canyon. Don has promised fossils, and we have rock hammers in hand. The
path is a scrabble of rock debris, and Don stops to point out animal signs
that are officially called "scat." The children are amused that this means
animal poop and that it's an important way to locate and identify animals.
When they start looking, however, they discover rabbit scat. Don guesses
they're probably jackrabbit pellets, since cottontail droppings are smaller.
Farther along the trail, Tev locates what appears to be coyote scat as well as
some bird droppings on the cliff face.

The low cliff surface is made up of different layers of rock, some crumbly, some hard. Don shows us what to look for, and we dig out loose pieces
of rock. We gently crack open the clumps, and sure enough, embedded
in the rock we find small rounded shapes of hard material: trilobites. Not

all of them are perfect, but distinct outlines make the markings identifiable. What a reward! Our discovery brings more questions. What are these creatures? How did they get here? How long ago? Once more, the ancient lake comes alive in our imaginations. It must have thrived with primitive creatures like this. I close my eyes to envision these dry hills covered with greenery, perhaps even a forest. So much history is in these rocks.

> DON: *I hold a rock-hard shrimp fossil in my hand and think about the desert shrimp that swim out in the muddy water of the playa. Those live shrimp are nearly identical to these fossils. The lifeline goes back so very far. It's a testament to the vigor and persistence of these creatures and their adaptability, the watchword of desert life.*

Amy keeps digging; she hopes for another fossil. Nate finally puts down the rock hammer and starts chasing lizards. I walk on a little farther. I reach out to brush away debris from an outcropping, and a small piece of the rock face moves. Startled, I step back as something flutters upward and flies past me—a bird, a poorwill. What perfect camouflage, exactly the same color and texture of the rock! I am excited to see it, but I don't see it for long. It lands on the cliff face down the canyon and is instantly lost to view.

We eat our sandwiches and dried apples in the shade of the camper and marvel at the ability of life to survive in such a forbidding landscape. This valley is not absolute desert, but it is close to it. The sage and saltbush are low-growing, and grasses are sparse. In spite of that, or perhaps because of that, it's a good place for wonder. We have encountered the strange, the unexpected, the surprising, and even the incredible. The children ask questions and poke at everything. Curiosity is rewarded. They find tiny trails and bird tracks in the sand, play tag with lizards, follow a large beetle with no obvious destination, watch a bug fall into an ant lion trap, and scare up a jackrabbit who hides in a thicket of grass and sage. Would that all children could experience such wonder, for wonder leads to knowledge. Knowledge leads to understanding. Understanding leads to greater appreciation and protection. In the case of the natural world, it leads to wise use and conservation.

> DON: *Saltbush and shadscale grow alongside sagebrush in this flat basin. Tough and hardy, they indicate extremely arid desert conditions. A food source for Indians and pioneers in early days, seeds are nutritious and young leaves and shoots taste salty. I find a few clumps of Indian rice grass, also an ancient food source. Cattle love*

it too. It's easy to overgraze arid land like this. Before cattle were
brought in, the Indian rice grass was abundant.

The delicate balance of life is easily damaged in the desert. Every wayward action scars the landscape and affects desert life. Lack of water diminishes vegetation, the basic food supply. Shelter is limited; survival is tough. Limitations have triggered enormous variety in the adaptations of plants and earth forms. Don calls it diversity, but I call it creativity. Is it just random luck? Is it ordered? Who can say for sure?

We are doing a bit of adapting ourselves; every camper or outdoorsperson does. We have pared down our lifestyle and equipment to the essentials. We have simpler daily routines, and we maintain basic supplies of food, water, shelter, transportation, and clothing. Don ensures that we keep warm in cool weather and have comfortable sleeping arrangements at night. Life in camp is different all right, but I love it. Simplifying the daily routines leaves me time for outdoor activities and exploring with the family. We get fairly creative when faced with new places and situations, especially home repairs or weather dilemmas. The limitations are good for us.

I squint at the colors and try to memorize them. In the blazing light of midday, color washes away to form a strong contrast with the bold shadows of rock outcroppings and dark crevices in the cliffs. Like the basics of desert life, the monochromatic color scheme is limited. One or two colors make up the subtle variations. Even sounds are limited. I walk away from the family chatter. A bird calls out faint tinkling notes, probably a horned lark. A rock falls from the cliff and lands with a soft *chuff*. Dry grass rustles in the afternoon breeze. Nothing else breaks the prolonged silence that lays upon the land.

As I pick my way around the sage clumps, my awareness shifts. The silence expands. The vast, empty playa no longer feels empty. Negative space is pervaded with something invisible and present. This awareness is new and yet not quite new. In fleeting moments when brushed with this sensation, I have ignored it. Today I find it hard to dismiss and even harder to define. I am held in the moment, and in the quiet, I listen. The afternoon wind grows stronger, disturbing the alkali dust. I turn back toward the others. Inner questions scatter to the horizons. What does this mean? In spite of myself, I have made some kind of connection.

Back at camp, a sense of awe is still with me. With watercolors I try to capture the subtle playa colors on paper. My color memory has improved, but tube colors are only approximate. I paint watery blobs of buff, gray, and off-white. What an artist calls "value" seems to be what the whole picture is about, light to dark. In art class I struggled with the concept, but here, with limited colors, the differences are obvious. My color values are automatic. The lakebed is stark white, the cliffs are a buff, dull brownish-yellow tan, and the clefts in the rock are dark gray. Somehow expressive of the solitude and silence, the color values set the "tone" for my small desert study.

I put down my brush. The desert is a perfect setup for wonder, which in turn leads to discovery. Stripped of non-essentials, spiritual awareness grows. Looking outward connects with looking inward. Values become clearer. I have to admit to myself, the desert is changing my perspective.

Soon I found that I was actually caught up in this new world,
and in some extraordinary way it began to teach me about my own self,
and about my place in the whole cosmic pattern of the universe.[1]

1. DeWaal, *Lost in Wonder*, 8.

Woods Lake, San Juan Mountains, Colorado

5

The Rocky Mountains, Colorado
San Miguel River and Woods Lake.

Patterns, pink elephants, and proportion

DON: *On our way to Moab, but it's a cool day in red rock country. We detour into Arches, which suffered a cloudburst yesterday. Roads washed out, and some tenters too. Weather breaking up today, and colors are intense. I take a number of evening shots of cliffs and monuments. Attend a good geology talk at campground.*

Next day, we sightsee and take photos. Head south on U.S. 163 to Utah 46, then turn east toward Colorado. The road goes up all the way; we climb about 4000 feet in twenty-five miles. Into Colorado on Highway 90 through Naturita, Norwood, Placerville, and finally find Falls Creek Campground, about twelve miles west of Telluride.

The San Juan Mountains rise from the Colorado Plateau and beckon to us for miles. After days of desert heat, I can't wait to see cool green forest. I am already painting small studies of water—that is, what I remember of places I've been. I am ready for cool colors, cool temperatures, moisture, and more abundant plant life. The fishermen are ready too, and we stop at the first campground.

DON: *Fall Creek sign says "No Vacancy," but I drive in anyway and talk them into giving us a spot. Four-wheel group from Arizona had* *reserved all the spaces. Set up the trailer and drive up to Telluride. Beautiful town setting with peaks and cliffs on three sides. Many old buildings still in use are designated National Historic Landmarks. Town is quiet mountain living at this time, since mining has dwindled, and not much in the way of ski resorts. Tev and I buy out-of-state fishing licenses; Nate is still too young to need one. Last year's price $10, fish limit of ten. This year the price is $25, fish limit of eight. Back at camp, Nate and Tevis go fishing right away and catch a few in the San Miguel River.*

Tevis is first to the water, pole in hand. Nate is close behind. Looks like fish for supper. We stay in the RV park for a couple of days for major cleanup, showers, and laundry. At the Laundromat I catch the local gossip and fishing information. A neighbor tells me that the dirt road up the canyon leads to "the most beautiful lake in the world." The next day we drive up there. That lady was right.

How do I describe something inexpressible? Eden comes to mind. Morning sun filters through the aspen and spruce woods that surround the lake. We park near a fringe of open meadow that graces the hillside. The children run down to the water, but Don and I walk into the meadow and up the hill. We are knee-deep in wildflowers and blooming grasses. We walk into the aspen woods and are soon wet to the knees with morning dew. So many species grow here: butter-and-eggs, Indian paintbrush, wild aster, sticky geranium, and the prized Colorado columbine, with its silver dollar-sized blossoms of blue and white.

A short trail leads back to the lake. We climb over an old split-rail fence flanked by spikes of pink elephant head flowers. I bend down to view the mass of delicate miniatures. Each bloom on the spike looks like a tiny pink elephant head, minuscule trunk and all. The detail is exquisite.

We walk around the north end of the lake to size up fishing possibilities. Thick conifer forest and stands of aspen extend down to the water. The upward slopes frame two snow-covered peaks, one on the left and one on the right. They must be 12,000 to 14,000 feet in elevation. We are close to the top of the world.

We can do a lot here—photography, sketching, fishing, and enjoying the mountain's beauty. However, the camp setup is not good right now. With no camping regulations in place, pickups with campers and trailers have crowded the available sites. Such a place is not meant for big rigs. Too many feet have trampled areas around the lake. This place is being loved to death. Is anyone else concerned about this? Fair use and conservation are needed here. We will have to come back later.

> Don: *Woods Lake overcrowded, so we drive back to the RV park. We take the trailer up the San Miguel River, set up camp about a mile above Ilium.*
>
> *We go fishing up the river. My dad taught me: "Choose a fly that resembles what's fluttering over the water. Keep out of sight and strip enough line off the reel to toss the fly out ten to fifteen feet onto the water. Let it drift downstream until you either catch a fish or the fly sinks. Then pull it out, step back into an open space, and whip the flyline back and forth to dry the fly. When it will float again, go back to the stream and try again."*
>
> *I try flies here all afternoon, but in the end I have to use eggs. I catch three nice ones, all on salmon eggs. Tev catches something else. A tree swallow zooms out and catches his worm just as it hits the water. Tev pulls in his line, unhooks the bird, and it flies off. On the way back from fishing, I take a couple of pictures of the Rockies at sundown.*

My field equipment now fits into a Boy Scout backpack, which accommodates a twelve-by-fifteen-inch Masonite board (Don rounded the corners for me); Arches brand of 140-pound watercolor paper; four sturdy clips to hold the paper to the board; a small roll of drafting tape (similar to masking tape except it won't damage the paper); two old soup cans, one large and one small, for water; a water bottle in case I'm not near a spring or creek; tubes of watercolor paint; my Allman watercolor palette in a waterproof bag (the ten-inch, round, white plastic palette holds twelve daubs of tube colors and has two large mixing areas in the center); a bamboo placemat rolled around several brushes; folded paper towels; a small elephant sponge; a pencil box with HB, 2B, and 2H drawing pencils; a brass pencil sharpener; erasers; one ballpoint pen with permanent ink; and a waterproof poncho for when I sit on damp ground or to wear in case it rains. This bare-bones assortment is lightweight and easy to carry. My small foldup stool is handy for sitting if there are no flat rocks or logs.

Painting by myself makes for one discovery after another. My painting classes set me up with basic equipment, basic techniques, and the rudiments of composition, but this is different. With no instructor hovering nearby, I'm on my own for deciding subject matter, how to compose, how to handle the water, which colors seem right, and which equipment works in different situations. I make my own decisions here—sometimes for the better, sometimes worse. For starters, my instructor recommended pigments that don't fit most of the natural colors I see outdoors. I need an art store when we get to town.

While Don and the children fan out along the river, I sit on my art stool and study the stream. My first attempts at painting don't look like water. I do have the right colors for the river: Prussian blue washes into Windsor purple along the edge where the water deepens, while a bit of Hookers green reflects the grass on the banks, and lighter blue in the center mirrors the sky. The problem is that my river doesn't look flat, and it doesn't flow. I study the San Miguel. I note the lines made by the moving current and how they elongate into graceful curves. Many of the lines are parallel to each other, curve for curve. I pick up watercolor on a fairly dry brush and imitate those curves. I work sparingly, "with economy," as my art instructor said, so as not to overdo it. With just a few curving lines placed in a logical direction, the water flattens out visually and appears to flow. Hurray!

I prop my painting in the sun to dry. I step back and take a good look at it. Those final curving lines look familiar. It was at the coast, the curving tide lines along the beach. That's not the only place. I remember the California sky the day we left home. Ice clouds in the stratosphere appeared as long, flowing lines gracefully curved into a long, lyrical rhythm. Aha! Flow patterns are formed by elements that move in a continuous stream, such as water, air, and molten earth. This simple discovery makes all the difference. Curving flow lines add necessary detail for this painting. What other patterns are needed for water? There must be more. I pull out a little notebook and start a list.

> DON: *No one camping near us on the river, although another camper is in sight about a quarter mile away. Have had very little rain in the Telluride area, but it frosted the last two nights. Today we are up at 6:30 a.m. to take the boat up to Woods Lake. The heater in our new trailer is very nice.*
>
> *Fishing on Woods Lake slow at first, wind very strong. Tev goes bank fishing. Nate and I have a great time rowing the boat around. It rows easily, even in the wind. Catch two nice trout on flashers and a little worm on the end of the hooks. After a couple of hours, we have six or seven fish between twelve and fourteen inches long. Nate lost what probably would have been the largest so far.*
>
> *Birds seen at Woods Lake: tree swallows, Western Sandpiper, robins, and flycatchers. Fish caught are rainbows, brooks, several cutthroats, and a German Brown or two. Wildflowers: lots of golden*

glow, purple asters, white daisies, and Colorado columbine. Trees around the lake are narrow leaf cottonwood, aspen, blue spruce, willows, and others.

While Don and Nate fish from the boat, Tevis hikes around the lake. He wants to fish in the creek that feeds the lake. Book in hand, Amy comes with me to explore the meadow.

"Hey Mom," she asks, "when do we start school lessons?"

I reply: "Not until summer vacation is over. Just like home, September is when school starts."

She is such a reader, she'll have read ten books by then. She will miss her school friends, but Nate is ecstatic that he gets to skip the seventh grade year. We'll cover the material of course, but teachers back home encouraged us to take this family trip. Children, and adults too, learn so much more from travel than can be found in a book.

Amy wanders off as I pull out my art pack. I'm drawing flowers today in this wild garden. I choose a clump of purple asters. Measuring with my eye or the length of my pencil, I compare the size of one part to another and place dots on the paper for guidelines. The proportions of each flower intrigue me, and each one is unique. I rough out general shapes and contours with light, sketchy lines. I can still hear my art instructor: Are the stems curved or branching? I pause midstroke. Is branching another flow pattern? Water flows inside those branches. Something to think about.

My inner art instructor goes on: Are leaves opposite each other or alternate, or are they basal? What is the basic shape of the leaf—oval, triangular, rounded? Are leaf edges smooth, serrated, prickly, spiny? Are stems smooth, hairy, thorny? What is the basic flower shape—round, tubular, oval? How many petals? What should I actually draw, and what should I only suggest? If I do this right, I know the eye of the observer will put it all together.

Don: *We troll over to the other side to find Tev fishing the lake; evidently no fish in the creek. Bank fishing here is not easy, it's too brushy, heavily forested, and steep. Suddenly Tev gives a big jerk on his line. The rod bends and jerks—sign of a fish too big to pull out of the water. He yells at us to hurry and get the net. I look down into the water. It's a whopper and securely hooked. "Beautiful fish!" I yell. "What are you using?" He yells back, "Stop talking and net my fish!" I put the net down in the water, and just to give him a bad time, I pretend to miss a couple of times. I finally get the fish up, and he really hollers. I estimate it's a three-pound fish a good twenty-two or twenty-four inches in length. A beauty.*

We row over and pick him up, then head back to the dock, pull the boat out of the water, and put it back on the truck. A good fishing day. Nate and I caught our limits. Tevis only caught one, but it's so big it is equal to all of the fish Nate and I caught put together.

Amy settles onto a flat rock by the lake to read. I move to another good spot to work near a stand of aspen. Their characteristic black scars contrast vividly against their smooth white trunks. Some knots and scars in the bark are from damage caused by animals or storms. The theatrical gestures of lower branches beg to be drawn. What artist can resist?

Aspen leaves flutter in the slightest breeze and whisper to me as I sketch. It's hard to believe aspen are called "trash trees" by inexperienced developers. Hardy and tough, aspen are a pioneer species, meaning they are often first to grow on barren mountain ground. Aspen have saved many a slope from erosion, which contributes to maintaining the water table in the soil. Their graceful presence signifies water and life.

I study the branching patterns. Like a fork in a river, the limbs branch off the trunk in a certain way. I pull out my small notebook and add "branching" to my list of flow patterns. That's when I remember branching was the topic of a drawing lesson. I can still hear my instructor: What is the relationship of limb to trunk where it branches? Does it curve up, angle down, reach straight out? What happens where the branch actually connects to the tree? What is the proportion of branch placement to the main trunk? Is it regular, irregular? I am back to proportion again.

Drawing is all about relationships: comparing one part to another, then comparing the parts to the whole by assessing size, angle, placement, space, volume, or degree. Right proportions make for harmony, a right relationship and a desirable one. If I render correct proportions as I place the lines on paper, then my drawing of the aspen trees will look right. I can't help but think this is a lesson for person-to-person connections as well. We can all work on right relationships and seek harmony in how we live.

I sketch and paint aspen and wildflowers most of the day, but overall what seeps into my awareness is the light. Today's atmosphere has been suffused with a soft light that shimmers. Filtered by mist in the early morning and later by cumulus clouds, it is a moist light—a blessing light. Colors mellow. Edges are slightly less distinct. Because of daily rains and morning dew, everything has a shine, a certain splendor. I pause from my work. I take a second look at this haloed world. Indeed, it seems hallowed as well, set apart. That thought sparks a dim memory: "set apart" is what "holy" means. Is this place holy? I quickly put that thought aside. I'm not yet ready for faith talk. That's been a closed subject for a long time. Instead I sit quietly to absorb the light and life that shines in this place. Whatever is going on, I love it. I want to belong. I want to be part of this beauty.

Beauty is the gift of God.

—ARISTOTLE[1]

1. Qtd. in Kaplan, *Bartlett's Familiar Quotations*, 79.12.

Waves on the San Miguel River, San Juan Mountains, Colorado

6

The Rocky Mountains, Colorado
Fishing on the San Miguel and Telluride

Trout for breakfast, turbulence, and Tomboy

WE CAMP ON THE San Miguel River for about two weeks. Amy fishes right alongside the men and catches her share. I cook trout everyday, sometimes for breakfast, often for dinner. No one seems to get tired of it. Here's how we do it:

COOKING TROUT

To begin, start with well-cleaned fish (the fisherman's job), and cut off the head. Fry strips of bacon for flavor and to render the fat. This saves on the camp supply of cooking oil. Roll the trout in cornmeal, salt the inner cavity, and fry it in bacon fat, first one side, then the other. Fish is done when skin is crispy and falling apart and the meat is opaque, flaking easily with a fork.

To eat trout, first discard the skin. With a fork, gently lift meat away from the backbone along the line of natural separation that runs the length of the trout, first the lower half, then the upper. Watch out for small bones in the upper portion. If the fish is well cooked, the meat will easily pull away from all the bones. If not, the diner has to deal with a few little bones, but it's worth it. After eating the top layer, the uncovered backbone can be pulled away in one piece, starting at the head. Enjoy the delicious meat.

A tip for kids: If any little bones stick in the throat, eat a small piece of bread. That usually takes care of the problem.

DON: *No frost last night, lowest temperature was thirty-six degrees. Somewhat cloudy this morning. Around noon, it rains hard and keeps it up about an hour with lightning and thunder. It has been sprinkling ever since, and it is now about 2:00 p.m. Country sure needs this rain. Humidity is about 35 percent. We stay in camp all day. We finish recording a letter tape to the grandparents. I repair the trailer, then put up coat hooks and a towel rack. Stabilize the boat on the pickup so the wind won't blow it around on top.*

The rainy season is upon us. It's a good thing too, since the area suffers from drought. I love the morning cloud buildup into sky towers of cumulonimbus, all mist and vapor. The shapes form and re-form as they build ever higher. I study contours and try to get them down on paper. On this trip, my drawing pens are drafting pens. The ink flows well, although the line width is somewhat static. I have to change pens to get a thinner line or a thicker one.

Drawing is a solitary task, but it's quiet and peaceful. The brain goes into spatial mode, a different way of looking at things. The *perception* shifts as the right side of the brain is activated.[1] No longer do I think the names of clouds, I think shapes, contours, edges, and shading. I see more fully, like an artist. Words fade away. I can't talk and draw at the same time. If anyone speaks to me, I reply with "What did you say?" I have to put down my pen and literally shift thought from images to verbal language.

DON: *Cloudy and rainy this morning. Good breakfast. Work on the boat carrier. Rains hard for a few minutes about 1:00 p.m., which forces cessation of work. We come in and are now eating lunch.*

It's 2:15 p.m., and the sun shines intermittently. I take the crew fishing and photographing up the San Miguel. I take several shots of the Rockies in the rain. I must get a map so I can name all the peaks. When I get around to fishing, I discover that Nate and Tevis have taken all the eggs, the only thing the fish seem to bite on here.

Clouds roil and flow, a great turbulence on high. On the top edge of rounded billows I notice wispy vapor that curls into waves, actual waveforms like ocean waves. Aha! I pull out my notebook and add "waves" to

1. Edwards, *Drawing on the Right Side*, 4.

the flow pattern list. As I watch, the wavy edges continue to reshape into more billows of cloud. Reminds me of what happens to cream when poured into coffee or the froth and bubbles on river rapids. This is riverbank chaos theory. Turbulent clouds appear disorganized, very disorderly. However, even through the disorganization the turbulence tends to form patterns. Here I can see distinct patterns on the cloud tops: wave forms, wispy curving flow edges, and rounded forms. Hmm. Is "rounded" a flow pattern? I have to think about that.

> DON: *Horrendous lightning storm in the night, and finally rain. Met the neighbors from Fullerton, California. He's a Jeepster and knows all the trails around here. Go to Telluride to do laundry, spend the day there. Telluride has been taken over by the hippies, but at least the town has a strict dog law. At the hardware store I buy one hundred feet of wire and a push button. I need to hardwire the electronic camera shutter release. Yesterday lightning triggered my radio control release on the camera and ran through a whole roll of film non-stop. City Park has campsites and water. We fill the water cans. It's good water.*
>
> *Telluride was originally called Columbia, but the Post Office objected because of Columbia, California, an older town. Since the mineral tellurium had previously been found at Cripple Creek, Colorado, it was assumed it would be found here, hence the name Telluride. One old native told me that only a trace of the mineral was ever found, and that was high up. The boarding house on the cliff was actually a power station; employees lived there. I take photos at the end of the canyon beyond town.*

On the way to town, Don pulls off the gravel road and parks. The fishermen jump out and walk to the river to scout out fishing holes. I lean against the camper truck and scan the hillside for wildflowers or signs of animal life. Overhead a couple of ragged clouds race over the ridge. One cloud is shaped like a gigantic flag, brilliant white, whipping in tremendous wind. It shapes and re-shapes as the ragged edges curl, then wisp away to nothing. The second cloud surrenders to the wind and sails onward. This one remains, a dazzling banner cloud furling and unfurling as it expands with great heroic gestures and radiant splendor. Where are the trumpets? This is a herald, for what? The morning? The light? The majesty and joy of—what? Something bigger and beyond, that's for sure, this time beyond beauty. For an artist, beauty is the ultimate. What is beyond beauty?

I call to the others. We stand in the deserted road and watch the cloud. Don pulls out the camera to take a photo, but ultimately the full effect of light and restless movement cannot be captured on film. We gaze in silent wonder until slowly, slowly, the cloud majestically glides away over the ridge. Awed by that heavenly banner, we climb into the truck and drive on.

How can I possibly paint such an image? It was more than cloud, more than beautiful. It seems presumptuous to ask, but was this what the ancients called *glory*? The dazzling light, the stunning image? My perception shifts. "What is beyond beauty?" may be the wrong question. The beauty of this cloud invites more than a "What?" It invokes a different inquiry, "Who?"

> DON: *The main course of the San Miguel River originates in the mountains above Telluride. We are camped on the south fork, also called the Lake Fork because it runs out of Trout Lake. We drive up the Lake Fork to photograph. On the other side of the river, there is quite a large whitetail prairie dog town. These prairie dogs are curious; I can't get very close to them, but I stand right in the middle of their town and they pop up out of their burrows to watch me. I am able to get some pictures with the telephoto before rainy weather drives me to fishing instead.*
>
> *Catch some nice trout. Only miss my limit because I forgot the spare leader and lost one at the sixth fish. The kids are collecting rocks at an old prospect hole. They get some interesting quartz crystals.*

I find a place along the river where the current surges around rocks. I sit down to draw the wave patterns. Water pushes against a rock, not quite submerging it. This causes small waves on each side that break into foam. The foam curves around both sides of the rock and trails off into the current like two ribbons. When viewed from the road above, every rock is decorated with dancing foam ribbons. These particular rock and wave combinations appear characteristic of this river. Geology, water depth, and the angle of the flow no doubt shape the water currents to make this unique look. Do rivers have imprints? An intriguing concept.

Drawing the splash of wave and foam requires rounded shapes, even and uneven. Water drops tend to roundness, branching out in every direction from a common center. Hmm. A radial pattern. I pull out my notebook and add "radial" to my flow pattern list.

> DON: *I drive up the west side of Lake Fork to "Prairie Dog Flat" and spend from 9:00 a.m. to 4:30 p.m. trying to photograph whitetail prairie dogs. Not much luck at a good shot—a case where a*

fixed-focal length lens of around one thousand millimeters would be good. Must work on that.

While I wait hours for the "dogs," a bit of luck walks by. The small telephoto with the motor drive is already focused on a dog hole about one hundred feet out. The wire end and I, plus my large telephoto are in the back of the camper. Suddenly, a long-tailed weasel appears from under the truck. He disappears into a dog hole, which gives me time to shift the camera and focus on the hole. Shortly he pops out, hesitates in a perfect pose, and I snap the photo. He hears the click of the camera, but it does not frighten him unduly.

A day in camp. Here is my chance to draw Sunshine Peak. I find a spot for my stool over by the sheep corral in the meadow. Tevis is off fishing. Nate and Amy play badminton. Sunshine Peak sits serene in the morning light. As I draw, I marvel at the curves and jagged edges of the rocky cliffs and graceful sweep of forested slopes. Different shades of green show patches of aspen or conifers, as do subtle changes in shape and texture. I use the black drafting pens again. That is, after I clean them up. These drafting pens don't like changes in altitude. Every time I open them up, I find they have leaked India ink—pretty messy for travel. The morning flows by. The sketch begins to look like Sunshine Peak. An idyllic setting. Peaceful.

> DON: *We go four-wheeling to Tomboy. A narrow steep road, a real cliffhanger. Jan is scared all the way. Tomboy was an amazing mining operation, especially for the 1870s. The huge mining complex perched on a cliff way above timberline. Find some nice ore samples, and I get a fine picture of a gray pika. Not a rodent, it's in the rabbit family.*

We start up the Tomboy road early in the day before too many jeepsters are abroad. Hewn out of the rocky cliff on the east side of Telluride, it's a one-lane, rocky climb. A literal cliffhanger! In four-wheel drive, we bump and hump over sharp rocks and time-honored ruts. I am on the passenger side, the cliff side. I hold my breath. As we bounce along, I can see over the edge all the way to the bottom. Great view, but oh my! After a long, slow climb we make it to the top, thankfully without meeting anyone, so we don't have to use the narrow turnouts.

The incredible view stops us in our tracks. Snow-capped peaks surround us in a cirque of jagged sawtooth mountains, the backbone of the North American continent. The U-shaped basin is glacier-carved, a high mountain valley with elevation around 11,000 feet. The air is thin and sharp. A small creek runs through the area, eventually finds the cliff, and tumbles over the edge. Mine tunnels run deep into the earth here, and signs of old diggings color the slopes. Even though the Tomboy mine buildings were torn down in 1925, weathered gray boards remain strewn where heavy winter snows collapsed other structures. We are above timberline, but wildflowers peek up between the boards, and pikas whistle at us from their rocky perches on the slope. One bold pika stands sentry on a rock pile close by and watches every move we make. Don takes its picture.

I try to imagine the town as it was originally. People lived here through the winter, even some wives and families with children. Housing meant a two-room shack for Harriet Backus, the Tomboy bride,[2] who braved primitive conditions in the early 1900s to live here with her assayer husband. Bitter cold and heavy snows isolated Tomboy in winter. Food and supplies were hauled up that treacherous road, and gold and silver were hauled out. Strings of pack mules did the hauling; horses pulled freight wagons and sleighs. Coal and wood were brought up for heating and cooking. Water was scarce in the wintertime when all the springs and lakes froze. School was held during the summer months.

The Tomboy bride detailed her cooking attempts at such high altitudes, a challenge for baking bread and boiling any food. Ice cream was an easy dessert—just put the ingredients in a can out in the snow and stir it once in a while. Thawing frozen meat was difficult. On one very special occasion she prepared a roast dinner for company officials. After the normal cooking time had passed, she served the browned and crispy roast only to find it was still frozen in the center!

We sit on rocks to eat our lunch of sandwiches and dried fruit. The afternoon clouds begin to build. Another jeepster passes us and waves as they head on over the pass to the other side of the range. We pile into the pickup truck to head back to camp.

The return trip is worse. Downhill! We can see a couple of four-wheel-drive rigs coming up the cliff road toward us. Rule of the road is the driver headed downhill must back up and use the pullout. It's safer than the other car backing downhill, not so easy to lose control. We meet the first pickup, and Don must back up. I jump out of the truck. This trip is not for the faint-hearted! He deftly backs into the closest pullout, which is right on the edge of the cliff. I hold my breath as the wheels come within inches of the precipice. The other driver waves and grins as he goes by. I can't bring

---

2. See Backus, *Tomboy Bride*.

myself to climb back in until Don has pulled away from that precarious turnout. Thank goodness the next jeepster has already pulled aside and waits for us to pass.

We proceed down the rocky road. Even at a snail's pace, we are thrown from side to side, bouncing and jostling each other. The kids holler from the back. The porta-potty has broken loose from its moorings and bumped open its cupboard door. With the downhill tilt to the truck, it bounces and slides forward along the aisle between the bunks. Did the Tomboy bride have such a ride in the freight wagon? I can only guess.

When a banner is raised on the mountains, you will see it,
and when a trumpet sounds, you will hear it.

—ISA 18:3B NIV

House of Many Windows, Mesa Verde National Park, Colorado

7

Canyon Country, Colorado
Mesa Verde National Park

Ruins, rhythms, and rightness

DON: *August. We break camp and leave the Telluride area. Drive over Lizard Head Pass, down the Dolores River to Dolores and through low hills to Cortez. Buy food, propane, and hardware. Drive on to Mesa Verde. We have trouble finding a campsite. The campground is almost full.*

We are rained out of the mountains. Afternoon showers soak everything. The rainy season is to be expected, but soggy tents every night? That doesn't work. At any rate, it's time to move south. Tevis has to fly home soon.

After we stock up supplies in Cortez, we drive east to the park turnoff. Carved out of the side of the sandstone mesa, the road is a long, slow pull uphill into ancient times. Spanish for "green table," Mesa Verde is a good description for this not-so-flat-topped plateau that rises above surrounding hills. Shortly after the Christian era began, an ancient people, the Anasazi, moved onto the mesa and lived here for over a thousand years. I marvel at the thought.

The Anasazi were potters, weavers, and farmers, and by AD 1150 life was good on the mesa. Food was in surplus, potters were prolific, and the art of weaving developed in response to the quantities of cotton that came into the area by trade. The good times didn't last, however. Something happened, and massive mesa-top homes were abandoned as people moved into cliff-side caves and amphitheaters.[1] In the years AD 1200–1400, people moved away, leaving behind what they could not carry. Ruins of cliff dwellings number over six hundred in the park alone. We can't wait to explore.

> DON: *Spend the first day visiting roadside ruins. Once back in camp, we drive to the store and Laundromat. Jan starts laundry. Everyone takes showers. Good thing we saved all those quarters.*

We pack a lunch and drive the mesa-top roads. We stop at turnouts and tourist sites. Where permitted, the children clamber over and around rock walls. Don photographs. I find shady places to sit and sketch, building the old walls on paper stroke by stroke, stone by stone. I love the subtle sandstone colors and the visual warmth of yellow ochre, buff, and Indian red. It's like painting a sunset captured in stone.

Don remembers coming to Mesa Verde as a boy, when the road was a long, windy dirt track. At that time, the ruins were wide open to the few who came. He was able to crawl through room after room at Cliff Palace and even found remains of pottery. Now a flood of visitors comes from all over the world, and important ruins are roped off to protect the sites.

Life for the Anasazi was in precarious balance here. Dependent on annual rainfall for crops, their irrigation system used catchments for rainwater. They planted small plots of beans and grains, and in later times they also harvested corn, squash, and melons. They hunted and gathered native plants. Not an easy life, yet the Anasazi endured. Was it lengthy drought that drove them away? Invaders? I kick up bits of pottery in the grass, and farther on I see displaced wall stones, the thousand-year-old debris of an amazing culture.

> DON: *Spend another morning visiting ruins. The kids went to Long House this afternoon, but Jan and I are staying in camp to rest. We have good drinking water from a spring in the area. Water is life in this arid country. We will fill our tank here.*

We gradually fall under the spell of Mesa Verde, listening to its ancient tales and Indian lore. We pull into one of the viewpoint parking areas along the Cliff Palace Loop Road. Don grabs his camera, and I rummage for my art pack and folding stool. While the children explore, I carry my pack

---

1. Mays, *Ancient Cities of the Southwest*, 84.

and stool over to the rim of the canyon and set up to draw in the shade of a juniper. Across the shrub-filled gorge, a sheer cliff is marked by a row of small black rectangles. Mortared walls block off a sandstone cave that forms a little house with windows. It's probably one room wide and three or four rooms long. The ancient dwelling clings to the cliff. Access looks difficult, maybe impossible without expert rock climbing. Ancient paths have been washed out by weather, but hand and footholds might still be found in the sandstone.

An intermittent breeze stirs the rabbitbrush and ruffles bunches of Indian rice grass. I glance over my shoulder. Cultural memory is strong here. I have just settled down to draw when a sudden ruckus downwind startles me. A raven abruptly hoists its sails and rises out of a piñon. With loud raucous caws and its big black wings pumping, it soars out over the canyon. I watch it glide and bank near the cliff dwelling. It tacks in the wind and rises higher to clear the ridge. Then silence.

A sense of mystery pervades the area, and I am drawn to the solitude. The quiet and the mystery spark questions. What's the meaning? What can I learn here? Where will this quest lead? I'm not the first person to venture on such a quest. A vision quest is part of American Indian lore. Not only in this group, but also in every culture, in every century, the unknown has attracted seekers and pilgrims in search of meaning, greater understanding, renewal, or a new life. Unexpectedly, here on this mesa, I find myself among them.

Descendants of the Anasazi are scattered throughout the Southwest. Origin stories abound in the various cultures. Some find faith in a Creator, and rituals attest to the use of prayer. Evil is seen as the imbalance between humans and the natural world. To put things right, one can seek harmony through rituals and ceremonies.

That strikes a nerve. Imbalance still happens. In modern times, our way of life is way out of balance. Too often we do not work *with* nature but *against* it. Perhaps that's one thing I sense here: cultural memory calls—get life back into balance.

I finish the drawing and hold it at arm's length to get a better view. The House of Many Windows, my sketch will bring to mind the solitude of this place, the peace, and the mystery. Reluctant to leave, I pack up my sketchbook and pens.

DON: *We drive to the museum area. I load up my camera pack with gear. Tev and I take off on a two-and-a-half-mile hike along the Pictograph Point Trail. See a number of sandstone formations, which we photograph. Some are miniature formations that show large-scale erosional features, but all in miniature. Photograph Tev in a tunnel of sandstone the trail goes through. It was formed by a huge sandstone block that fell in some past time onto other large sandstone blocks.*

Several people pass us since we move along slowly. Find a good wildflower specimen of prince's plume and an ant lion colony. Farther along, we come to more ruins and a bunch of ferns called cliffbrake. Lots to photograph. Several caves appear to be old living sites. One is quite secluded, hemmed in and protected in front by medium-sized—or large, probably for this country—Douglas fir. Tev forgot the canteen and has to backtrack along the trail for it.

Don parks in the picnic area, which is the old campground where we first camped as newlyweds in 1957. The view is still the same. So are the camp robbers, those greedy gray jays that are ever-ready to grab food right off your plate. No doubt these are the same trees too, since they are long-lived. I walk down to the campsite where we stayed. In those days, we had a blue VW bus Don had modified with a bed, closet, icebox, and storage. We'd bought a new Coleman stove and some Army Surplus gear. I trusted Don's judgment and experience from his boyhood years of family fishing trips, exploring, and Scouting. This was the familiar country of his childhood, but all was new to me, and what a marvelous initiation into the wonders of the natural world! I was like a dry sponge soaking up the vistas, history, colors, shapes, and textures of the deserts and mountains we traversed. We honed our road trip skills, roughed it at times, fell in love with national parks, and reveled in the joy of living outdoors. Somewhere along the way, I bought my first small watercolor pan, brush, and drawing pad. That was the beginning. Since then, summer camping trips have continued to expand our sense of place, even our very sense of being, and raised more questions: How does this work? What does it mean?

Don and Tev take off on their hike; I dig out lunch for Nate, Amy, and myself. We joke about being out here on the "liager." That was somebody's Scrabble invention for "a dry land peninsula." The joke was that we believed them because they "read" the definition aloud from the dictionary and fooled us all. Now here we are in the perfect place, one that seems like a liager because the topography of Mesa Verde spreads out in fingerlike projections of land that are separated by deep, narrow canyons. No wonder the park has such long, windy roads. Major plant cover is piñon pine and some ponderosa. In this campground area we have a juniper, piñon, and mountain mahogany forest, while sage, rabbitbrush, service berry, and other shrubs grow on the more open ground.

The three of us eat lunch on an old picnic table. I sketch for a while, then explore with the children. Even in this developed area of park buildings and traffic, it is possible to kick up pottery shards in unexpected places. The sky clouds up and threatens rain. We cross the road to go to the museum. What is this? Right behind one of the buildings we find a field of stones, each about one-and-a-half to two feet across. They lay like a giant puzzle in the dry grass. Pentagons, hexagons, and a few four-sided chunks make up the pieces. An ancient mudflow must have covered this small field at one time and then hardened into geometric shapes. I reach for my notebook and add to my growing list of found patterns—not flow patterns this time but stationary geometric shapes.

> DON: *Tev and I are obviously going to be late meeting Jan and the kids by two o'clock in the museum parking lot. Still, we saunter on. Clouds thicken overhead; it looks like rain.*
>
> *We arrive at Pictograph Point, where there are some first-rate Anasazi pictograms chipped in the rock face. This is about halfway along the trail. From here, the trail crawls up the cliff and onto the mesa top. By now it is sprinkling. Common sense tells us to stay down in the canyon where there are plenty of shallow caves for us to wait out the rain. But we decide there must be small overhangs near the rim on top and trek onward. There aren't. So much for logic. We find some protection under a big juniper tree. After waiting some time for the rain to stop, we finally walk the mile back to the museum in a light drizzle.*
>
> *When we reach the museum, the sun comes out. I photograph the unusual rock formations Jan found behind the museum. Looks like sandstone that hardened from a fossilized mudflat, all geometric patterns. I have never seen anything exactly like this before, and here it is, right in back of the museum. Nobody walks through here much, I guess. Later, we head back to camp to record a letter tape for the grandparents.*

We drive to Balcony House. Don and the children take the tour. Since I have been here before, I take advantage of time to sketch. I am still thinking about balance and imbalance when I spot an old juniper, itself an artistic composition worthy of any gallery. Twisted and gnarled, marked by weather and age, this grandfather tree dominates the area. What is noteworthy is the precarious balance. The strain of long years on this rocky plateau shows in a dramatic lean to the left. Around the old-timer, younger trees grow straight, fairly evenly balanced on all sides, symmetrical. My art instructor would be pleased to use the old juniper as an example of asymmetry. Roots are no doubt anchoring its precarious position.

I sketch the pattern of parallel stress lines in the exposed wood where the bark has worn away. The lines curve upward around the trunk. In this one tree are examples of the two types of visual rhythm: flowing movement and recurring pulse. The flowing movement shows in curving stress lines like a lyrical melody or a dancer's line captured on film. In the second type of rhythm, an element recurs at regular intervals like the beat that underlies music. Here it can be seen in the repetitive placement of branches, needles, and berries that punctuate the contours of the central trunk.

I am dealing with art principles here: rhythm, pattern, and balance. It is arguable where one leaves off and the other begins. My inner art instructor speaks to remind me that art principles work together. I marvel anew at the complexity of earth, this great work of art. Every art element and principle is present, no matter how insignificant the form. Principles of order hold things together, like this tree. Any imbalance in systems—interruption of enduring rhythms, broken cycles, disruption of life patterns—all these harm relationships and cause disorder. Continuing disorder harms life.

The lesson on balance gives me another piece of my composition puzzle. It's still on my mind when I hear voices. The hikers are back. They climb up from the Balcony House cliff and straggle into the parking lot. It's time for me to load up, but the questions continue. Human culture equates balance with justice. Doesn't that equate to right relationships in human affairs? Fairness, equal treatment, equal opportunity? What does it take to insure a just life? Can we build a life of harmony with ourselves and others? No time for discussion as I readjust my pack. At any rate, some questions have to be lived; the answers don't come all at once.

Perhaps that's the message of the old juniper. For long years it has been a major contributor to the give and take of life in the mixed aspen/juniper plant community. Visually, the very form of this forest elder demonstrates a stability that has endured. The gesture is one of dignity. Weathered surfaces mark a certain wisdom. Artistically and biologically, the balance is just right—it works.

I step past the juniper and trip over a stone in the grass. Gravity is ever to be reckoned with; I nearly lose my own balance.

See, I lay a stone in Zion, a tested stone,
a precious cornerstone for a sure foundation . . .
I will make justice the measuring line and righteousness the plumb line.

—ISA 28:16–17 NIV

Landscape Near Echo Amphitheater, New Mexico

8

Canyon Country, New Mexico
El Morro and the Rainy Season.

Lunch stop, first rain, and lightning stories

DON: *Head south into New Mexico. Arid landscape but beautiful. Shiprock dominates the area. The old volcanic core is called the Rock with Wings. Ancient folk myth says the rock was once a great bird that transported the ancestral people of the Navajos to their lands here in northwestern New Mexico. They fled from a warring people near what is thought to be the Bering Strait. Shiprock has been a major pilgrimage site. Young men make solitary vision quests in the area. Just driving past somehow lifts the spirits. Must be the shape and the height.*

Shiprock is visible for a long ways. The solid silhouette is a bold state-ment that stands out on the horizon, mesmerizing in its isolation. We stop for a photograph or two. I feel a strong sense of the unknown out here, like something is stirring. The sense of space is mind-expanding.

We drive on, and at lunchtime we pull into a wayside picnic area. We carry sandwich makings over to a table near a piñon pine tree. The presence of any tree indicates water, but the area looks dry, dry, dry and still awaits the rainy season. The children explore nearby, itching to take the trail over to the sandstone bluff. It's the base of the monolith that rises up out of surrounding countryside, a land filled with pine, oak, and sweet-smelling juniper. This is El Morro, Spanish for "the headland," an ancient oasis where the sandstone cliff shelters a surprisingly large pool of water. The result of summer rains and springtime snowmelt, the pool is a centuries-old waystop and a dependable water supply for wildlife, native peoples, and wanderers.

The tree that shades our table looks dry and dusty, but its roots go deep to tap into the water table. I admire the textured bark and old scars from lost branches and wish for time to sketch. I call the children back to eat as the first cloud blots out the sun. A sudden breeze whips through the piñon needles and dusts our lunch. Restless air swirls up small spirals of plant debris and dirt into miniature dust devils. Aha! Spirals. I make a mental note for my flow pattern list.

We eat hurriedly with an eye to a sky, which is filling with clouds. Is there time to walk the trail to the pool? I want to see the inscriptions carved into the sandstone. As early as 1605, before the Mayflower landed in New England, Spanish explorers found this oasis, and ancient peoples scratched petroglyphs long before that. A gust of wind flings sand our direction. We grab for flying napkins and paper plates. The children dash on ahead as Don and I clear the lunch table.

I am last on the trail as the wind grows stronger, blows more leaf litter, and ruffles desert shrubs. I notice curving flow patterns in the dust as it whips along. Here come the others, already backtracking to the truck, but I tie down my hat and keep going. The air is electric, which a huge crash of thunder confirms. Rain is coming, and the very earth is alive with the news.

I duck into a shallow alcove to look for inscriptions. In spite of the wind, the air grows heavy with moisture. To my wonder, something indefinable, like a low-level yearning, rises from the ground as dormant plants awaken with desperate thirst. Crosscurrents of air lift, then swirl away to rattle dry sage and rabbitbrush. Wind eddies flatten dead grasses that line the trail. Palpable longing hovers in air that is so charged with expectation I can almost hold it in my hand. My mouth goes dry.

I dash toward the pool. A cottontail rabbit scurries across the trail. I hurriedly scan for inscriptions and gaze at the pool, which holds the remains of last season's water. A crash of thunder up on the mesa loosens huge drops of rain that splash my path. I stretch out my hand to catch a raindrop. Parched earth and thirsty life exhale yearning and need. Moist air quivers with promise and hope. Thirst, yearning, hope, promise mingle in electric communion that enfolds the pool, the cliff, the trees, the underbrush, and etches deeply into my very bones. More drops hit my hand, scattering dust and stirring up the intoxicating aroma of rain. The sweet, moist fragrance fills the air, then with one more thunder crash, the storm breaks. Pelting rain pours from the skies.

The path is rapidly awash, and so am I. I run for the trailer. *Thanks Lord. The land thanks you, plants thank you, all life thanks you. I thank you.* I shake water off my rain parka and hang it up to dry. When was the last time I prayed? I cannot remember, but this was spontaneous. Today it burst forth as the only fitting response.

The deluge continues, soaking everything in sight. Before long, water is running off the cliff. We can't see from here, but the chute above the pool must be a waterfall by now. Water streams across the bedrock close to the trailer. It forms little rivulets across bare soil and drains in the direction of the wash. Flash flooding is a distinct possibility.

The sheltering piñon tree almost dances with wind-tossed branches, its wet needles shining. What a miracle water is: life-giving rain, a great blessing. The washes, streams, and rivers spread the blessing. I envision water collecting in pools and lakes, making reservoirs for wildlife and people. Ground water seeps deep into aquifers for long-term supply. My family and I are bound up with this water cycle that sustains life. It's a unity of need, source, and supply. What a marvel!

> Don: *El Morro deluge. Never have seen such a downpour this close. Miniature flash floods on all sides. We will wait it out.*

While we wait for the storm to abate, we pass the time by telling lightning stories. Not one of us can forget the trip some time ago to the North Rim of the Grand Canyon. We watched lightning strikes across the canyon just fifteen miles away. I was sketching on a rocky point as wispy clouds drifted haphazardly toward us but still some distance away, we thought. Don and Nate were photographing along the rim. Without warning, we heard the buzz, felt the electric surge, and Amy's long hair stood on end. In an instant, we were on the trail running. That was too close.

One story leads to another: Two years ago at Chaco Canyon, we were camping in our tent trailer. We had spent the day marveling at the ruins—skilled masonry, patterned stone walls and doorways, and especially Pueblo Bonito, an extensive crescent-shaped structure of many rooms, apartments, kivas, and dwellings. How did they haul those huge ponderosa logs from so far away? Why the layout of straight roads, still barely visible, that radiated to long-forgotten places? How? Why? Always the mystery.

The main event of that memorable day, however, had begun after supper. It was too warm for an evening campfire, so we sat around the picnic table and watched the sky. Like a night at grand opera, the evening darkened. On the distant horizon, dry lightning flashed and clouds began to billow and roil. Expanding in our direction, ominous and turbulent, they rumbled closer and closer. Aggressive wind, lightning stabs, horrendous thunder. "One, one-thousand, two, one-thousand, three, one-thousand," we counted from flash to rumble, trying to judge the distance from camp. The monumental storm built up and boiled overhead with spectacular flashes of power and light that raced from cloud to cloud. The very air crackled. The thunder grew deafening, felt primeval. Alarmed, awestruck, scared, exhilarated, we huddled at the picnic table with no shelter at hand except the tent trailer, which was totally inadequate. I flinched with each lightning bolt and covered my ears at thunderous roars. For over an hour trees thrashed in the wind as the tumult increased. Then, without fanfare, the drama shifted. Fickle air currents swirled dust around our camp and changed direction. Like an ocean liner leaving port, the monumental storm cloud slowly pulled away, growling and flashing. The whole storm system headed east, running lights flaring. Lightning lessened, thunder quieted. The massive cloudbank shipped back toward the far horizon. Awed and shaken by the power of the storm, we sat in silence. The night was warm, and I remember that not one drop of rain fell that night, far different from this El Morro deluge.

> Don: *El Morro has a high sandstone cliff with a plateau on top. Sage, rabbitbrush, Indian rice grass, and other grasses scatter through the area. On the flats, Yucca with its cream-colored flowers is mixed in with the sage. Piñon pine and juniper grow on the hills and plateau. Agave abounds in the sage on the hills. Agave has yellow flowers and likes rocky places. Both plants have edible fruit. Earlier, along the road, I stopped to photograph buffalo gourd. Handsome leaves and egg-shaped gourds, creamy-white with green stripes. A very useful plant. This rain is something else; I can't photograph in a storm.*

The rain lets up. We close down the trailer and head for Santa Fe. I roll down my truck window to smell the air, sweet with moisture and the strong scent of wet sagebrush. Ditches run with muddy water, and a thin flood has washed across the highway in places. This is high desert country, fairly arid, with lots of geologic formations and some lava outcrops mixed with rangeland. I imagine early Spaniards riding horseback through unknown territory. With a pack animal or two, they rode these very ridges, skirted canyons, sought water holes, and negotiated this rough but passable country.

I can't sketch while we travel, but my eyes sweep the landscape. I absorb the lines of lava cliffs and memorize the colors of grass and sage, the silhouettes of trees, and the contours of hills and distant mountain ranges. The drive allows time for reflection. My mind wanders back to that spontaneous prayer. Where did that come from? I had long ago given up talking to God or even acknowledging God. My difficult teenage church experience left scars. Not that it was all bad, just bad enough. Fiery stories of hellfire and damnation put a cloud of fear over everything. A tide of fundamentalism surged through our small congregation. A follow-the-rules legalism crept into the teaching—no joy, no fulfillment, just fear of judgment. This was not good news. The negative culture bred a poverty of spirit. I wanted out.

We cross another watercourse, a steep little canyon that still runs with muddy water in the bottom. The straight-sided walls could be lava or sandstone, and they channel the water in time-honored curves and incomplete S-shapes. After the rainy season, the creek bed may end up as dry as the one I saw last year at Chaco. That one was a mass of dried mud plates all curled into geometric shapes, mostly five-sided. They were fragile pentagons of the previous season's mud, my first glimmer of earthwork order.

So what is my thinking now? I try to imagine a Creator. How would such an Artist work? How does the Genesis story go? Like any major art project, it starts with the idea, "in the beginning." The Creator worked with light, mass, and space in a masterful economy of means to make sky, water, and dry ground. As every artist knows, the work develops as you go along. In this case, first the physical world, then vegetation, then days and seasons, then animals and humankind. The whole effort was masterfully coordinated within the limitations of time and space.

And accidents? Murphy's law? Anything that can happen will happen? What my naturalist calls "opportunism?" Every artist learns how to take advantage of spilled paint, drips of water, or a slip of the brush. Unplanned events are cause for greater creativity in making something out of the mess. And for better or for worse, the creation at some point takes on a life of its own. What comes to mind is the garden of Eden and its two willful caretakers, Adam and Eve. I chuckle at that. Events didn't exactly work out according to the original plan.

We drive on toward Santa Fe, where Spanish and Pueblo Indian cultures meshed in the 1500s, a long time ago. After weeks of camping, civilization appeals to all of us. Art galleries and bookstores beckon. Museums and history walks await. Best of all, we have tickets to the Santa Fe Opera.

And these are but the outer fringe of his works;
how faint the whisper we hear of him!
Who then can understand the thunder of his power?

—JOB 26:14, NIV

Lichen Rock, Haviland Lake, San Juan Mountains, Colorado

9

The Rocky Mountains
Santa Fe, Haviland Lake, and Silverton

Art on the go, color studies, and radiance

Don: *Santa Fe. Rent a space in the Vagabond Trailer Park four-and-a-half miles south of town. At $5.55 a night, it's one of the least expensive we've found. Clean swimming pool, clean laundry. Excellent water. The park is crowded, but it does have nice tall shade trees. Spend the day seeing Santa Fe and charging the trailer battery. Can't find a good hardware store.*

The sky, the sky! What blue is that? Cerulean? Azure? Mountain blue? High-altitude light crowns the morning. No wonder artists come here to paint. We find paintings everywhere: stunning murals in the downtown Santa Fe Post Office, museum exhibits of Taos painters of the early 1900s, and shows of contemporary New Mexico artists like Georgia O'Keefe, who is a legend in her own time. We troop through museums and art galleries. I discover the etchings of Gene Kloss and instantly identify with the style, the drawing, the subject matter. She depicts landscapes I have seen and loved. Artistically, I claim a kindred spirit.

Don: *Last night we went to the opera. At first pelted by hail and rain in the open-air theater. Wore ponchos and probably smelled a little fishy. The opera was* Marriage of Figaro, *an excellent production. Laughed until my stomach hurt.*

In Santa Fe, we walk the downtown history loop. Don acts as tour guide, reading brochures and leading the way. We hover over Indian crafts displayed on sidewalks, tables, and inside shops. I love the rugs and pottery. Nate admires Kachinas. I am thrilled to see the cathedral that is central to Willa Cather's story of Santa Fe's first archbishop, who arrived in 1850.[1] Amy is more interested in the swimming pool at the RV park. She is finally brave enough to swim in the deep end.

> Don: *Tev caught the plane in Albuquerque. We miss him already. Back at camp, we spend all day working on the pickup and trailer, cleaning plugs in the pickup. We put in a new Protector III; I also install a new water pump in the trailer—it's now very quiet. The spark plugs still do not work, so Nate and I find an auto parts store and buy new plugs and wires.*

The last evening in Santa Fe, we emerge from the grocery store loaded down with our bags of groceries and look up to find a wondrous sky. A spectacular sunset in the west spreads its glow across the dome of the heavens and reflects in full glory off the eastern cloudbank. Billows of coral, pink, and lavender light up that edge of the horizon. What a show! We hurriedly load groceries into the truck and drive to the first roadside view area. Don pulls out the camera gear and sets up the tripod. Resplendent heavens bloom with color. Luminous orange puffs are backed by maroon rainclouds that show off the brilliant pinks above. Colors flame. Clouds churn. Radiant pastel tints contrast dark indigo depths that threaten rain in the mountains. A cloud curtain of gray-blue sky-fleece draws aside to reveal a misty half-moon. We are spellbound. What a beginning for our fall adventure. Tomorrow we head for the Colorado Plateau in search of autumn colors. The journey is all about color.

> Don: *September. Drive north to Taos, then take U.S.-64. Cross the Rio Grande Gorge, 680 feet deep, very impressive. On to Chama. Lovely drive. This is the high Rocky Mountain area of northern New Mexico. On through Chama to Pagosa Springs, then Durango. Very pretty drive—a long one for us at a distance of 220 miles.*
>
> *A spark plug wire keeps coming off during the trip, so I have to stop and make a new one. Fortunately, I have the materials. We rent*

---

1. See Cather, *Death Comes for the Archbishop.*

a space in United Camp Ground two miles north of Durango. The
Denver and Rio Grande narrow gauge train goes right by our camp.

It is already time for school to start. We dig out spelling and math books. Lessons begin for Nate and Amy. Daily assignments include writing a journal and working up science projects out of the field guides. When the train whistles, we drop everything and run to see the old steam engine and passenger cars chug past on the way to Silverton.

I have my own assignment. My classroom palette doesn't fit what I have been seeing. The student pigments are not true to this landscape, except for an occasional wildflower. The colors are too bright. The sage, junipers, conifers, rocky outcrops, and distant mountains all challenge my color sense. Western outdoor colors are more muted, even earthy. I ponder new choices.

> Don: *For some time, the trailer weight has been bending the rear*
> *bumper. Now the metal connecting the bumper to the chassis is*
> *tearing. So today I shop around Durango for a load leveler—find*
> *one for $225 designed to fit on a truck. It will fit around the spare*
> *tire and has a ball of adjustable height. I order one. We head north*
> *to Haviland Lake, where we are now camped in the Forest Service*
> *campground. Our new hitch will be installed next Wednesday.*

Camp routines work well. Here we have a good campsite with a spot for the pup tent, so the children sleep out. If it turns cold, they can move into the camper bunks. Sleeping bag, pillow, and duffle bag are basic equipment for them. Rolling up clothes makes it easier to retrieve them from the duffle with fewer wrinkles. Before we left home, Don built Nate and Amy each a wooden box with a lid for storing assorted treasures. Nate's bunk box holds books and a souvenir or two, but mainly his tape cassette player, earphones, and a stack of classical music tapes—mostly piano. Amy stores dearly loved books and a small rock collection. Sunrise, her well-traveled Indian doll, resides on the bunk pillow.

> Don: *Spend the day fishing in Haviland Lake. I get my limit of*
> *medium-sized trout. Haviland Lake does not allow motors, so our*
> *rowboat is great fun. Not much in the way of fall color here yet. The*
> *camp has good drinking water.*

I pull out my paints and set up on the picnic table. Amy joins me with her colored pencils and paper. She lines out and decorates a colorful September calendar for the trailer—a good idea, since we tend to lose track of the days. At first, getting away from a nine-month school schedule seemed like freedom, but we find ourselves on another sort of schedule: a trip to town every week for groceries, gas, supplies, a stop at the Laundromat, and good fresh water to refill the trailer's water storage tank. When camping, we tend to save good tank water for drinking and use creek or campground water for dishes and washing up.

I experiment with colors. What suits this landscape? I work wet-on-wet with different blues and reds. Aha! Prussian blue and cadmium red mix into a useful Payne's gray that works for storm clouds. More versatile than straight tube color, mixed colors may separate on the paper or shift in value, which makes interesting combinations. Controlling it is another matter, but this gives me two primary colors for outdoors. I still need a yellow.

> Don: *Last night it rained fairly hard. Today it drizzled all day. I write most of the day. Late in the afternoon, Nate and I take a hike to the east of our camp. We can hear the train whistle of the Denver and Rio Grande narrow gauge railroad. The Animas River is over there too. We never see the railroad, but we find a large wooden flume that still functions. We walk along the catwalk on top of the flume for about a quarter of a mile. On the way back, I photograph a crusty lichen attached to a large rock at a forty-five degree angle. It is beautiful in design and subdued in color, a blue-greenish gray. It measures almost a foot in diameter. In camp, I study up on lichens. Lichens grow very slowly. This specimen must be at least three or four hundred years old, maybe more.*

Not many campers in the campground here. We are lonesome a couple of nights, then an Australian couple pulls in with rental car and trailer. In a short time, we are fast friends. They potluck with us at our picnic table. I proudly offer biscuits baked in my little trailer oven. She reaches for one, then points out that we need a butter knife for the butter. Hmm. Well, we are pretty informal out camping, but I dash to the trailer to find something akin to a butter knife. When properly appointed, we dine. We enjoy the biscuits while serenaded by murmuring ponderosa pines and the music of whispering aspens. Later, around the campfire we roast marshmallows and regale each other with travel stories.

A large outcropping of black rock streaked with quartz dominates one campsite, and I sketch it one morning. The quartz pattern is reminiscent of flow patterns, a tantalizing geologic event. These mountains have held plenty of ore. Spent mines dot the slopes. Aspen trees by the lake have not yet turned color, but we are only about 8700 feet in elevation. Higher on the mountain and across the lake, the aspen trees look orange, not yellow. Don thinks the color is due to drought conditions. In spite of summer rains, the West suffers from a three-year drought. The lake is surrounded by forest, and all of it is very dry.

> Don: *Spend the whole day photographing. Although it's late in the season and summer is over, flowers still bloom vigorously. We row across the lake to get a photo of a beaver. Every day, he sunbathes on an old dead tree that has floated out into the lake. Nate rows the boat to within fifteen feet of the beaver, who rears up looking disgusted and dives into the water. I can't get a clear shot because of the branches. The beaver smacks his tail at us, splashing water with two very loud thwacks, then paddles away.*

I delve into the art books I found in the Taos bookstore and read about the color theory of J. W. Turner, the great English painter (1775–1851).[2] Instantly I am in over my head, but here is food for thought. Every painter *en plein air* ponders the phenomena of color types: *reflective* or *refractive*. Sorting out the two is a puzzle for me at first. Everyday objects reflect color from the light of the sun. I rarely think about that; it's just the way things are. Reflective colors depend on the primaries of red, yellow, and blue plus any mixes or dilutions.

The colors of light itself are the refractive colors. The light spectrum colors clouds, sunrises, light beams, time of day, and atmospheric effects. Photographers deal with refracted light, well-illustrated when projecting color slides. Rainbows display the light spectrum with a set of basic hues: red, orange, yellow, green, blue, indigo, and violet. Seven colors like a musical scale of seven different notes. The octave, a repeated color, may be said to establish the overall tonal family of rainbow colors, perhaps similar to framing a musical scale with a particular key tone. It certainly expands the meaning of color harmony. I marvel at yet another parallel between art and music, that of color and tonal harmony. It's a unifying factor. These analogies are brainteasers, but the math doesn't work out very well. Secretly I'm glad that such beautiful phenomena remain mysteries.

How can I use this? Turner worked at painting atmospheric color effects, especially in his late watercolors. I study book examples, examining sketches of ocean, shore, and atmosphere.[3] His transparent colors are layered and blended in all sorts of ways. The seaside mists and fogged land-

2. See Gage, *Color in Turner.*
3. See Selz, *Turner.*

scapes evoke a certain otherness.[4] In fact, in these paintings he is reported to have been striving for an expression of spirituality in the world rather than painting an actual scene. The sublime grandeur of the natural world became evidence of the power of God—a theme that other artists and poets explored during the same period. The significance of light was linked to God's spirit, and Turner's "impressionistic" late paintings show such light effects, especially in his depiction of atmospheric radiance.[5] Obviously, I have ventured into an old and continuing conversation. Other painters before me have sensed mystery beyond the physical landscape. Turner's wet-on-wet brushwork required practice, a keen eye, a skillful brush, and without doubt, a bit of luck.

I take my art pack down to the lake boat ramp and find a place to paint. I pick up my brush and experiment. So much is involved. The breeze ripples the water in an all-over pattern of dancing lights. I make a mental note to add ripples to my list of patterns. The breeze strengthens and the ripples line up into parallel waves. The forest is dark green. The dry grass has a special pale yellow color. Can I make them look right on paper? Still looking for the perfect yellow to complete my triad of primary colors for outdoors, I pull out a tube of raw sienna, one of the earth colors. It looks right for the dry grasses on the bank. I try mixing raw sienna with Prussian blue. That turns into a rich forest green, perfect for the conifers around the lake. Aha! I have found my yellow. It works well for this landscape.

> Don: *Spend two days in town getting the trailer hitch put on. Not all of it arrives from Denver, although it was supposed to. Got home late the first day and had to go back.*

First stop in Durango is the bookstore. Paperbacks are inexpensive, so we give the children a fifty-dollar limit and turn them loose. They pile up a grand selection, including favorite authors Elizabeth Enright and Madeleine L'Engle. This launches our reading program, along with Bible stories out of the Young People's Bible that Grandma gave them. We want them to be familiar with the stories. Don finds the Christian bookstore and purchases a Moffatt Bible. We are both reaching back to our roots.

> Don: *Leave Haviland Lake and drive slowly to Silverton, taking numerous photographs of the high Rockies on the way. The pickup acts*

4. See Gaunt, *Turner's Universe.*

5. *Wikipedia*, s.v. "J. M. W. Turner," accessed December 5, 2015, https://en.wikipedia.org/wiki/J._M._W._Turner#Style.

*up—as if it isn't getting enough gas. Altitude is 10,000 feet. I open
the hood and enrich the gas a little. Now it is running better. Stop at
a private camp in Silverton.*

*Frost this morning. Aspen are beginning to turn color. Spend
time photographing aspen. Jan paints. Aspen groves are a little dis-
appointing due to the drought. Finally we find a golden-yellow stand
of aspen just off the highway.*

Most of the day we drive the roads around Silverton looking for fall
color. Patches of yellow aspen beckon on the mountainsides, but most are
too far away or too difficult to approach. By midafternoon, we turn off the
main road on a dirt track that leads into the forest. After about a quarter
mile, conifers open up to aspen woods in full fall regalia. At last. Don parks
the truck and gets out his camera gear. He and the children walk farther up
the dirt road to photograph and explore.

With art stool and pack, I step into the aspen woods and enter a golden
wonderland. The yellow canopy reaches skyward, gold leaves shimmer on
every side, and my footpath is aglow with fallen leaves as sunbeams dance
through branches. The flood of golden light washes over me. Radiant still-
ness is disturbed only by whispers from the rich tapestry of leaves that still
cling to white-barked branches.

At first I stick to business and make color notes. The sunshine is re-
fracting light that casts a yellow glow. The leaves, tree trunks, rocks, and
path all reflect that light, revealing what artists call "local" color. I need
every different color of yellow paint I brought on the trip—golden ochre,
raw sienna, the cadmium yellows. How do I paint light that shines and
refracts? Reflective colors that dance before my eyes? I want depth to this
color, not just flat strokes on the paper. Layering might be the answer—yes,
washes of different yellows. And don't forget some contrast, maybe with a
complementary color. I paint some swatches, then draw a leaf or two and
render small color studies of the aspen.

Little by little, the radiance creeps into my bones, into my very spirit.
This shining cathedral casts a heavenly light that colors the air around me.
Sunlight sifts through glory-rimmed leaves. What is this about? I set aside
my paints. In an odd way, this reminds me of El Morro: the overpowering
storm, the electric sense of invisible bonds, the extraordinary interaction
that swirled around me and enveloped me. The rainwater that flooded from
the skies slaked a thirst I didn't know I had.

Here in the aspen I am inundated by a growing flood of light, a totally different sensation, yet once more, my inner artist is touched to the core. I came to paint, study color, and get it right on paper, but this is more than color, more than theory. In this hour of solitude, the plant community has come alive with blessing; it glows with light that lifts the spirit. This is celebration; whispering leaves applaud. An echoing sensation surges within me. Or is it from above? Am I in God's sanctuary?

A wondrous sense of love comes gently from somewhere beyond this forest—a love for all creation. Its gentle advance surrounds me, filling me until I feel my last wall of resistance melt to nothing. Time stands still. I soak up the brilliance, the radiance, and the wave of love that satisfies a hunger I didn't know was there.

The world is charged with the grandeur of God.[6]

6. Hopkins, "God's Grandeur," 128.

Grand Valley from Colorado National Monument, Colorado

10

Colorado Plateau

Colorado National Monument

Bedrock campsite, sculpture gallery, and life on the edge

Don: *Head for Colorado National Monument on the western border of Colorado. The monument runs along the edge of the Uncompahgre Uplift, part of the Colorado Plateau, which covers an enormous area. Land is semi-desert—piñon pine and juniper plant communities. We can expect ravens and jays, maybe even desert bighorns and, of course, coyotes.*

The road appears carved right out of the sandstone cliff that shapes Colorado National Monument. We gear down for the long, slow drive upward. At the top the road levels off, and the terrain turns into a novelty of bedrock with patches of vegetation. We find a campsite near the rim. The children burst from the truck to explore while Don and I level the trailer. Before long, Nate calls us over to the rim at the very edge of camp. The children certainly have developed an eye for photography. I catch my breath. Two thousand feet below us, the Grand Valley spreads out in a patchwork of farm fields and orchards. The flat, angular patterns stretch away to melt into distant mesas. Winding through the valley, the Colorado River carries Rocky Mountain water all the way to the Gulf of California. The distant landscape is colored with purple cliffs and mountain ranges as far as we can see. No transition zone here—we stand at the edge of our world.

That's not all. Amy points to the cliff face just below us. High relief stonework of free-form sculpture adorns the rim rock in convoluted curves and dips. Carved by storms, wind, and water, rock niches form small caves about as tall as Don, with some deep enough to step into. A narrow ledge provides a foothold. We step down and inch our way along until we can enter the first niche. Risky, but possible. We step around the sturdy sandstone columns of pure form that connect the cave floor to the rock roof. Aglow with earth colors in layers of creamy white, yellow ochre, and earth red, the columns look as smooth as wood turned on a lathe. I reach out to stroke a curving column, but it's not smooth. Instead I loosen grains of surface sand on the hard stone. Why am I surprised? The graceful form is in sharp contrast to the grainy hardness, yet somehow that solid core feels sure, right.

My senses are on the alert since my aspen woods epiphany. I take a long look around the small coral-colored cave. Are there telltale signs of the Artist? Fingerprints on the stonework? Did the Master Sculptor leave clues on these exquisite forms? Or perhaps the forms, the shapes, the colors *are* those fingerprints. Don goes back for the camera and spends hours photographing in this precarious spot.

> Don: *Campground very pleasant at this time of year. Good water, free firewood, no fee at this time, and no people. In the evenings, travelers do roll in from the freeway down in Grand Valley. View from our camp is outstanding. Clear view of Fruita below us and Grand Junction off to the right. The valley is another Eden with orchards, fields of row crops, horses, and cattle.*

Bedrock offers few places to stake the pup tent. Nate finally anchors it with rope to sage bushes and one picnic table leg. Amy suddenly jumps back, stamps her feet, and brushes off her pant leg. She stumbled over an anthill swarming with red ants, the kind that bite. Fortunately, she was quick enough to avoid pain. We keep our distance and watch the frenzied activity. The nest is a mound of sticks, dirt, and thatch with openings at the top. The chaos is organized and mesmerizing. Ants busily trail out from the nest and back in orderly files, bringing food gathered from various sources. In one line, each ant struggles with a single, large seed, hefting and dragging the cumbersome load. When Nate disturbs the trails with a stick, the ants move in slightly hysterical patterns, but they always find a way around the brushed area and back to the nest. Another wonder: the order and industry that sustains an ant community. The wisdom of nature offers a metaphor for life.

> Don: *We drive the Monument Road, a real cliffhanger. Hopefully, I am getting some fine pictures. We find a small canyon to explore. It's a slow walk due to photographing and painting activity. The kids explore every sandstone nook and cranny. Sandstone walls are too steep to climb. Not safe either, since coming down is always slippery with loose sand on the bare rock. When we get back to our pickup, we have a courtesy ticket applied to our windshield. I guess we parked in the wrong place.*

Don takes field notes for his sabbatical project. In most places, pines and firs grow at higher elevations. In canyon and mesa country like this, the vegetation pattern is reversed. Here the piñon and juniper grow on top of the mesas, while ponderosa pines and Douglas fir are found in canyons where the water supply is better and temperatures are generally cooler.

Rabbitbrush is in full bloom on both sides of the road, the fall flowers a mass of yellow—a perfect accent to the raw sienna color of dry grasses against the red sandstone. We pull off the road and wander on foot up a narrowing rocky canyon. Birdsong greets the morning and resonates between the cliff walls. The distant descending notes float on the air, haunting and pure as crystal. High overhead, little birds fly about the rim before diving into the canyon with a sweet call. Spiraling up again, they flutter around the rock crevices in a carefree and joyous party. We hand around the binoculars, listen, and check the field guide. They are unmistakably cañon wrens.

Don sets up his tripod to capture the crescent moon that hangs in the pie-shaped patch of blue sky above the canyon. The children climb the sandstone boulders. I find a flat one to sit on and pull out my sketchbook. The pure birdsong echoes again with a clarity that lifts the spirit. This is pure joy, a song to herald the morning. I wish I could hear it every day. As I watch the birds, my awareness shifts. Time stands still. The space around me fills with that now-familiar peace. It's like lifting a veil between the seen and the unseen world.

Grounded in time and place, moments like this are unplanned, yet they hint at the universal. What a gift—a sense of a spacious place, an infinity of peace. Poised for one brief interval on the edge of that space, I am aware of both worlds, each wrapped in wonder, rightness, and mystery. I sense two realities—not a mental imbalance, but a shift in perception. Yet I cannot hold the moment for long; it soon fades away. This short glimpse of otherness catches me by surprise. How to connect? I need a compass bearing, an orientation. Without thinking, my lips form a prayer, whispering long-forgotten words: *God is in this place—truly. And I didn't even know it!.*[1] *Thanks and praise. Thanks and praise.*

> Don: *We see few animals here. We scan the heights for desert bighorn sheep, but no luck. A coyote howled in the night; no sign of foxes or mountain lions. We make too much noise. Campground has a good share of rodents and desert cottontails. Nate is collecting insects. He captured a prize fly yesterday. Fall colors are muted here or non-existent. We are either too early (green leaves) or too late (no leaves) for good autumn color.*

Back in camp, I set up shop on the picnic table. The mountain range across the valley begs to be painted. Jagged cliffs and erosion lines sweep downward and define the base as it evens out onto the plain. I argue with myself about the lines. Should my brush strokes define the top of the ridge or the bottom of the washes? On the chosen range, the ridge tops are bare and light in color. Drainage washes are darker, probably full of vegetation. Paint what you see, says my inner art instructor. Where is the light? Where is the dark? The soil, minerals, color of vegetation, lay of the land, and the play of light and shadow make every hill appear different. Haven't I already seen every possible combination on our travels? I take another look and paint what I see. It works. I'll never forget this day, this place. My small study looks like the eroded desert hills. I am elated.

> Don: *Gambel's quail scurry across the trails when we walk around here. Today we saw a yellow-headed collared lizard sunning on a rock. They are so comical when they run. Have not seen the plateau whiptail yet, but it is found here.*

We wake to a change in the air. By mid-morning, we see the first cloud. As we hike to a red rock site, we keep an eye on the sky. Our panoramic view puts us right in the middle of drama. Clouds increase into great fluffy mounds, so like the rounded patterns I find in desert vegetation and in piles of red rock formations. The wind picks up. Flat-bottomed clouds sail on invisible layers of air as the upper billows pile higher and higher. The rain cycle is in life-giving performance today: evaporation, condensation, and the brewing precipitation. This moisture has moved north from the Gulf

---

1. Gen 28:16. The Message.

and now condenses into the clouds that fill the sky. They grow darker and more awesome by the moment, like primeval forces at work.

The ominous clouds form and reform in ever-larger masses, which make us feel smaller and smaller. Uneasy. The terrible beauty of the storm buildup cancels any sentimental feelings about nature. At one time, John Muir climbed a tall pine tree in the Sierras and held fast as he gloried in the power of the storm.[2] I'm not that brave. For all its magnificence, nature can remain indifferent, unyielding, and unforgiving. We need to take care of ourselves.

Lightning flashes on the horizon. Distant thunder rumbles our way. Sunlight and shadow shift, putting the spotlight first on one mist tower, then another. Mountain contours darken into silhouettes. Red sandstone cliffs take the stage in a momentary glare of sunshine.

When wind shifts our direction, we run for the truck. Not much protection can be found on this flat mesa. Powerful gusts literally blow us back to camp. We find the pup tent flapping wildly, but the ropes still hold. Amy chases my hat for me as Nate and Don pull down the tent and store camp chairs in the pickup. We take cover inside the trailer. Wind scatters loose debris across camp; utter chaos seems imminent. Another crash of thunder, then the deluge lets loose in a streaming downpour of rain and hail that pounds the metal roof. Our modest shelter rocks in the wind.

Don jokes, "Maybe we'll need an Ark if this keeps up."

The children agree, but I have a flashback of an old painting: a lake, a storm, a few panicky men calling on the Master. With disaster imminent, Jesus rebukes wind and waves; he calms the storm. The men marvel: "What kind of man is this?" they ask. "Even the winds and the waves obey him!" I make a mental note to re-read that story.

Red-brown water flows freely across the bedrock and into roadside ditches and washes. Rainwater threatens to flood the camp, but a final drumming on the roof signals a halt. The storm subsides as the clouds pull back and open sky reappears. Ragged, spent clouds drift on across the valley as the view emerges from the mist.

We wander the camp. Our gear is intact. We check on the neighbors. Their table tarp is down, but otherwise they are OK. Nate wades into the miniature flash flood that washes litter and gravel across our campsite. He hauls rocks to dam the flow of muddy water headed toward the cliff edge. He manages to hold back a shallow lake for a while until the dam

2. Muir, *Mountains of California*, 192.

gives way. The flood rushes toward the edge in a brown waterfall that takes small rocks, sticks, and other debris with it. Below the rim, the falling water—now a force of nature—carves stone, smooths it, and shapes contours before draining to the valley below. The river draws away the mud, and over time the flow will clear the water. The land makes ready for new life.

It's so quiet with the storm stilled. We are all safe, with only one small casualty: Amy's hairbrush. We can't find it anywhere.

He brought me out into a spacious place;
he rescued me because he delighted in me.

—2 SAM 22:20, NIV

Sand Dunes, Great Sand Dunes National Park, Colorado

11

Colorado Plateau

Black Canyon of the Gunnison and Great Sand Dunes

Canyon depths, humming dunes, and something beautiful

> Don: *Drive to Black Canyon on the Gunnison River. Find an actual forest of serviceberry. I have never seen so many in one place. Cold up here, nearly 9000 feet. Truck acting up—sprayed in carb cleaner.*

I get short of breath at the least exertion even though this camp doesn't look all that high in elevation. Nate finds wood and starts a campfire. Amy pulls out the jump rope and skips down the camp road. She is counting past one hundred when she comes back, and I make her stop to rest. It's easy to overdo it at this altitude. We walk the campground loop, which is empty except for one other car. Days are distinctly shorter now, and in the dimming light the mountain mahogany and serviceberry look nearly colorless, dressed in loden green and dull maroon with no oranges or bronzes ablaze with fall color. It must be the drought. The place is very dry.

Early in the morning, my wakeup walk takes me through the serviceberry forest and out to the rim. I emerge from the shrubbery where the earth ends. Dark cliffs with shadowed contours plunge into the chasm where a shining ribbon of river unfurls along the bottom. The black cliffs are rough and crumbly, older than recorded time. These metamorphic rocks are thought to be the sands, mud, and volcanic residue of an ancient sea bed. Under heat and pressure, they were changed over the ages to gneiss, schist, and other kinds of rock. Minerals are also found deposited in this earth crust.

The dramatic canyon shapes and shadows beg to be painted, but I have no time to get my brush wet. I study the descending contours, measuring with my drawing eye the placement of every curve and drop. I cannot shake the impression that I am looking back over eons of time. The ancient rock bears scars of cataclysmic upheaval, unyielding pressures, and long periods of erosion. The very depths are another wonder for my inner art gallery. The longer I look, the deeper it gets. Reluctantly, I turn back toward camp. It's breakfast time.

> Don: *Two days fishing on the Gunnison, then up the Taylor River north of Gunnison. Park in North Bank Campground. Very pretty, but weather cloudy and rainy. Try fishing, but no luck and no bites— don't see any either. I fished this river with my dad as a kid, and it was always an outstanding fishing stream.*
>
> *Second day. I walk far up a small side-canyon in the morning rain. Beautiful, but I get very wet. My new boots soak through. Find masses of kinnikinnick with red berries to photograph. Leave the rain on the Taylor and drive down to Gunnison, then up the Tomiche, south up the Cochetopea to the pass, down the Saguache, and on south to Great Sand Dunes. Weather lousy, although I do get some nice shots on the Saguache.*

A long, spreading stretch of land opens into the San Luis Valley, which instantly becomes my candidate for one of the most beautiful places on earth. Guarded on one side by the Sangre de Cristo Mountains, the sweeping vistas end at massive sand dunes that crowd the base of the mountain range.

It's hard to get perspective on the size of the dunes. My notion of dunes goes back to the coast where we started, but these dunes are 1000 feet higher in elevation than Pacific coast dunes. Unseen winds have sculpted contours in ebb and flow. Morning shadows define swales hollowed out by winter winds. The whole mass of dunes looks fluid, like turbulent waters that churn against the mountain barrier before flowing back some distance onto the valley floor to meet encroaching grasses. Two antelope grazing near the road lift their heads to watch us pass. They are not alarmed in the slightest.

We are high elevation here: 8200 feet. No wonder it's cold on this fall day. We back the trailer into a sheltered campsite. We barely fit, truck and all, but camp setup is quickly done. No pup tent here for the children; it's too cold. I grab my art pack and an apple, and we are on the trail out to the dunes with the children racing ahead.

> Don: *We hike out onto the Great Sand Dunes in the late afternoon. Meet a large-camera photographer out there from Castle Rock, Colorado. He's writing and photographing a book on the high Rockies. He invites Nate and me to go four-wheeling with him up Medano Creek tomorrow.*

Large spear and dart points have been found here as evidence of Stone Age people who came to hunt and gather. I imagine herds of mammoths and prehistoric bison grazing the grassy areas. What an image! We'll be lucky if we see an elk today. Don thinks they are higher up this time of year.

The sand crunches under my boots, feeling soft and hard at the same time. I lose all speed and stop to puff; the altitude is getting to me. My naturalist husband says the sand holds us back so that we will stop and look at everything. I take a second look. The height and bulk of the dunes loom dauntingly large.

Nate and Amy run ahead. They clamber up the first dune, then roll, slide, dive, and scoot every way they can. It's hard to get hurt here. Particles of sand move along the surface as the wind picks up. The sand makes an odd sound—a swishing, at times almost a humming. Dunes in this location are considered stable, but the wind and the force of gravity reorganize moving particles into wayward hills, hollows, dips, and mounds of sand. Over time, the whole bulk of the dune slowly shifts. I close my eyes to sense the wind and listen to the sand. For a brief moment, I feel part of the natural process of dune-shaping. It's an odd sensation that inspires me to hum along, although I don't think I find quite the same pitch. Does the whole earth have a song?

Here on the dunes, I find pattern after pattern traced on the sand. Flow lines grace the contours. Bird tracks record a winged visitor. I find insect tracks that seem to go nowhere. The sand slows even the beetles as they plow miniature canyons and leave a faint trail. In this unlikely spot a few hardy grasses are determinedly growing. Bending in the wind, the seed heads curve over far enough to sweep the sand and draw a complete circle around the plant—a radial pattern in the making. I pull out my sketchbook.

Don: *Nate and I drive up the creek with our new friend, Paul. We get into the timber, where we find lovely stands of golden aspen, spruce, and white pine. It snows on us up high. Paul puts a new dent in his Chevy Blazer by sliding into a rock beside the dirt track. Take a number of pictures. Get back to camp late in the day. We give him our book on wild edible plants[1] and head back to the trailer.*

A cold wind blows up a disturbance of some sort. Amy and I stay at camp and catch up on schoolwork and baking. My little trailer oven works well. Cookies are in short supply, and we mix a batch by hand. While Amy works on her math, I pull out my sketchbook and review my latest drawings and color studies. My work is evolving. My hand feels more sure when I pick up a pencil or a brush. The fluid sensation of hand and brush can be as exhilarating in its own way as singing. A certain release and a freedom goes with the strokes. Hmm. How do I maintain that facility when the trip is over and we go home? Daily practice. New routines. It's a must.

Beauty—that's the aim, making something beautiful. Individual drawings and paintings are only fragments of what's out here. I gaze out the window at the dunes and the dark mountains looming behind them. What a stark contrast in shape, form, and color. Not only the visual display, but also the abundant life found on the higher slopes with their tall conifers, high mountain meadows, and quaking aspen groves that are now patches of gold in the shifting sunlight. A rich community of life! It's high contrast to the barren dunes blowing down here in the wind. These glimpses of beauty rise up so unexpectedly in fleeting moments that touch the heart, only to slip out of my grasp, yet remembered forever.

Don: *Snowing heavily this morning, but it doesn't stick. Cold outside. Comfy in our trailer. In the afternoon, Nate, Amy, and I go for a long walk all the way to the top of the dunes. Quite a hike. One step up, half a step sliding back. It takes a while to get there. Design in the sand is quite outstanding. Dune grass turns out to be the highly adaptive Indian rice grass. An edible plant with a growth pattern that is taller and fuller than in the desert. Easy to see natural processes at work in the flow of sand grains, the action of wind and gravity, and the flow of water. Processes like cohesion—what makes things hang together—are so obvious where wet sand piles up higher than dry sand. The qualities of the sand material itself play a part in the process. It's a land-forming laboratory here.*

1. See Kirk, *Wild Edible Plants.*

The sand dunes are striped today. Uneven bands of dark and light sand decorate the slopes. The darker areas are moisture-soaked from rain and snow, but the lighter bands are already dry. The design is a mesmerizing art appreciation course right at hand. I regret disturbing the patterns as I walk; they are so varied and endless. This surely is another clue to the Creator.

I hike onward in the flowing earth. The dunes are constantly moving, and the patterns record their flow. I pull out my notebook and count the types I have found: curving flow, waves, ripples, spirals, branching, radial. I see examples right here in the curving flow of the dune contours, the wave pattern of the large dunes, ripples in the sand, branching weeds, plant spirals, and circles around the windblown Indian rice grass. Don names a pattern I have not yet officially observed: a meander. Not a meandering line that wanders away, this pattern is a specific phenomenon, a flow that curves back on itself in a continuing S-shape. Except for a moving snake, I have not spotted one. I'm on the lookout, especially around waterways. The small gorge in New Mexico wasn't quite a perfect meander.

> Don: *Today is a good day to get out on the dunes: light wind, intermittent sun. As time passes, the day becomes more sunny. Take many photographs. I find black gooseberries on the trail and then shoot dune scenes. Finally return to the trailer about 2:30. Eat a late lunch and go back to the dunes around 5:00 p.m. for the shadows. Shoot more pictures, which should be good.*

We cross Medano Creek to get to the dunes. It flows out of the Sangre de Cristos and onto the flats, where it disappears into the sand. We walk down to where it has spread out in shallow rivulets. We hop from dry spot to dry spot to get across. Amy turns aside here to play in the water. During the spring thaw, the creek floods wide and deep. In early summer, it's a great place for kids to play. This season, we notice the water flows farther over the sand in the mornings, but by afternoon, it doesn't go very far. Today it's almost warm in the sun with no wind. Nate charges ahead with the bug net. Don wants to identify the beetles on the dunes. I pull out my watercolors to paint a small study of dune contours, all shape and shadow.

My art pack is lighter than when we started this trip. I have pared down the brushes to a wash brush and my favorite Sumi trio with bamboo handles, watercolor pan, sketchbook, and a small board and clips for good paper. My art instructor would say I have discovered the other side of the coin of limitation. This is an economy of means, managing more efficiently with fewer materials. Economy of means is useful in all creative work. The simplest idea is the best. I am learning to use less in both color and composition to say just as much or, dare I hope, more? Surely this is the art version of Ockham's razor.[2] That medieval thinker must have been a Sunday painter.

> DON: *We get up before dawn, pack up, and take off. Some little distance outside the entrance station, we stop and wait for the sun to come up over the Sangre de Christo range. I set up two cameras for shooting the sunrise on the dunes. These should be nice shots. Cold this morning.*

We hang around the rig in the cold morning and watch the light change. Muted fall colors surround us here in a distinctive valley monochrome of dry grasses. Antique gold and pale browns contrast with the red earth colors and streaks of fall darks in the shrubbery and weeds. On the still-shadowed mountains, the swatches of dull gold locate the aspen stands. Nate walks out into the sage and grass and looks for lizards, but it is much too cold for reptiles to be out. The land looks a lot like desert, but those sage roots reach down to the water table. Not a true desert here, this area gets regular rainfall. I want to relocate to this beautiful valley until Don tells me how cold it gets in winter. Thirty below and wind? I don't think so.

A lot of history walked through here on horse and on foot. In early days, American Indian tribes hunted bison and gathered food in the area. Spaniards arrived officially with Diego de Vargas in 1694, although sheepherders and hunters from the Spanish colonies came before that. Zebulon Pike described the dunes in 1807, and explorer John Fremont arrived later. Most days, we don't find time for the social studies textbook, but at least the children are learning western history.

A faint wash of color slowly infuses the cloudless sky. Indigo night pales to a weak gray-blue that melts into lemon yellow, briefly mixing into a surprising tint of luminous green before the band of yellow gives way to coral blush. A heavenly artist shifts the rainbow palette as the sky slowly turns bright orange, then pink.

Even at this hour, the grandeur of the scene is overwhelming with the valley so wide, so long, and the mountains so high before us. My inner

---

2. Duignan, "Occam's Razor." The principle of economy or the law of parsimony ("It is futile to do with more things that which can be done with fewer") was recognized by medieval theologians, philosophers, and scientists. It was named after William of Ockham of the thirteenth century because he mentioned it so frequently and employed it so sharply in his works.

eye adds the fourth dimension—Black Canyon dark depths. The earth is so eloquent of beauty, so crafted, that is surely not an accidental invention. The sheer scope is another metaphor for something. What else compares? I love it all.

A narrow brushstroke of deep, glowing red edges the mountain peaks before a few rays of sunlight thrust above the ridge, casting long shadows forward in front of adjacent peaks. It's foreshadow. Amazing. I never understood the meaning of that word until now. When the sun rises into full view, the violet foreshadows shorten, then finally vanish. Sunlight brightens the sand to pink-beige. The dark forest now reveals green hues as the aspen lighten into bright golds. Low shafts of sunlight contour the dunes with indigo shadows. They slowly shift and reshape until the sun rises high enough to visually flatten out the contours. It's something beautiful to remember always. Something beautiful to cherish.

What a morning. Chilled and hungry, we walk back to the rig for a second breakfast.

And I pray that you, being rooted and established in love,
may have power, together with all the saints,
to grasp how wide and long and high and deep is the love of Christ.

—EPH 3:16–19, NIV

Old Barn, Frederick Farm, Akron, Colorado

12

Going Home

Prairie to Mountains to Mesa to Canyonlands to Great Basin

Don: *October. On to Cañon City. Spend time looking for a new tire. Over in the San Luis Valley, we caught a tire on a cattle guard and ruined it. No tire like that found here. Leave Cañon City late and drive the 120 miles to Denver. Visit the Denver Museum of Natural History and take the tour behind the scenes. We stay until the museum closes. I take forty-two pictures of the wonderful dioramas for my biology class.*

Nate and I go downtown to Eddie Bauer. I buy a down-filled field cap, camouflage color, and pick up watercolor paints for Jan at Meiningers. Then we drive to Longmont for the tire, which costs $98.50. We head for the farm tomorrow.

We stop to see Aunt Gladys and Uncle Willard in Denver. The children enjoy a lot of attention, and the Denver Museum is a hit. After three days, we travel eastward onto the ocean of prairie that rolls away into the distance. I love the heart filling, mind expanding space. The vast bowl of sky is a never ending pageant that extends to distant horizons so flat they appear truly horizontal.

This jaunt is a fast loop tour to see the relatives before we head home for the holidays. Days are shorter, nights are longer, it's time to move indoors for the season.

Most of the land around Fort Morgan is dry land wheat farming. Aunt Joyce greets us with open arms. Uncle George piles the family into the truck to go see his turkeys. What catches my attention is the field across from the house, which is irrigated land. Right now it's full of dried up corn, all shades of brown and awaiting harvest. I walk over to see the cornstalks at close range, so beautiful with leaf forms crisping in the fall sunshine. The beauty is in the detail. Long parallel leaf veins outline contours that curl downward at the ends, shaped and twisted by wind. Rarely are colors solitary; they are highly relational. Here the main color of rich medium brown has limitless gradations of tan and beige that flow from brown tones. The palette is monochrome, one color. Even as leaves wither and dry the beauty holds. It won't last long. In another day or two the field will be cut and gathered.

> DON: *Prairie farmland weather is warm, 82° F today. Air not very clear. Lots of dust from farmers working their fields, also smog from Denver. The prairie looks like fall with all the crops and wild grasses. Nothing much is blooming, but fall light shining on dead grass and mature crops like corn very photogenic. Birds are flocking up as they prepare to move south. Most cottonwoods out here at Fort Morgan show no sign of yellow yet, while the aspen in the high country turned color a month ago. Fall unquestionably in the air, the sunlight is very low.*

We drive on to the old family farm. The children are happy to sleep in a house again. Amy is at Aunt Eva's elbow in the kitchen. She chatters away about our adventures while she nibbles biscuit dough. Nate is outdoors climbing on the old tractor and other discarded farm equipment parked in the dry grass. Don and Uncle John talk crops and old times. It's a world apart out here. Peaceful.

I walk the dirt road next to the field. These colors are analogous, still with a common hue, but with added variety. I savor the beige and golden tans of dry grass that border the plowed field and the rich darks of newly turned reddish-brown earth. Furrows stretch away in long parallel curves that come together on the horizon. Some of these grasses are the exact shade of my new Gamboge yellow. The old barn leans badly, but the boards are a wonderful blue-gray. Barbed wire sags where a fence post collapsed. The clock on farm life here is running down, a natural cycle of its own. It won't be too many years before the folks move into town. Their stories are woven into a fabric of life in this place, as surely as the plants and animals that belong here. The life community prepares now for winter, the growing cycles complete. Colors of winter are gradually replacing the colorful fall palette with browns, pastel skies, and dark silhouettes. Nature's checks and balances hold the land secure.

> DON: *Heading west we drive to Montrose. Try to make it to Tel-luride, but gas supply to the engine gives trouble again. We spend the whole day getting car fixed, replaced the fuel pump. Drive on to the San Miguel with no gas trouble. Camp at the mouth of Silver Pick Creek. Aspen leaves are largely gone, but the narrow leaf cot-tonwoods along the San Miguel River are outstanding in their golden colors. Spend a day photographing.*
>
> *Drive up Specie Creek Road into relatively high country. Find aspen in beautiful deep orange and gold colors. This particular fall, they have turned color slowly, one golden bunch here, another bunch still green over there. Most have lost leaves by now, but these groves still retain the gold.*
>
> *High up on Specie Creek Road are large areas of Gamble oak, but none have acorns. Took many photos today of fall colors. Play horseshoes with Nate and Amy in the late afternoon. It is elk season, and the woods are full of hunters.*

Narrowleaf cottonwoods along the river are brilliant shades of yellow and gold. Warm colors complement the cool colors of water that mirror the clear blue sky. Along Specie Creek, I marvel at the deep maroon, bronze, and burnt orange combinations on Rocky Mountain oaks that form a rich autumn tapestry. I make quick color studies of the short trees. We drive up the creek road to find aspen. The tall, slender trunks are hung with clumps of color—a distinctive growth pattern for this particular forest. I am finally satisfied with fall color in the Rockies. Don has lots of notes for the Rocky Mountain portion of his study project.

> DON: *Leave for Mesa Verde. Hope to find some acorns there. Al-though open all year, 90 percent of the facilities are closed down. Jan is not well, so Nate and I go on the fourteen-mile drive down to the ruins. With a clear blue sky, I take a lot of shots of ruins and a couple of the canyons. Shiprock to the south is visible.*
>
> *Jan still unwell, so we stay another day. Nate and I drive to the ruins, and I photograph Balcony House. Back at camp, Jan finds acorns growing on the Gambles Oak around the campground! I take many shots of them.*
>
> *Temperature gets down to ten degrees Fahrenheit in the night. Freezes some trailer pipes, but there are no cracks. Take off for Canyonlands, a new National Park, driving through Cortez and then Monticello, Utah. Rent a trailer spot at Canyonlands Resort.*

*Campground very dirty, but the owner is a real character. In the
morning, we drive on over to the National Park Service campground.
All water around here, including resort water, has to be hauled in.
Nate and I go four-wheeling.*

Our sprint toward home has given us a road-rider review of the plant
communities Don is studying: prairie grasslands contrasted with Rocky
Mountain alpine fir and spruce as well as riparian neighborhoods filled
with stream-side cottonwoods in brilliant fall colors. Mesa Verde gave us
a quick look at piñon and juniper groupings with added Rocky Mountain
oaks. Now we head for Canyon country.

We pull into the new Canyonlands park. An enormous sandstone
boulder sits right behind our trailer. Bedrock outcropping is a better description. The children cannot stay off of it. Have rock, will climb. After
we get settled, I take another look. The sandstone surface is covered with a
mass of curving lines that flow around ample contours. No doubt a record
of stresses and strains when the rock was forming, or perhaps flowing water
laid down the sand at intervals—it is a prime example of the patterns I'm
collecting. I run to get my sketchbook and stool.

We are in the rain shadow of the Rockies here, so rainfall is not common. The soil is thin due to sandstone bedrock, and plant life is sparse. The
familiar piñon and juniper combination reigns with sage and salt bush scattered across the red earth. Nate and Don have a great time four-wheeling
even though on some tracks the pickup truck is a bit large and heavy for
safety. They turn back when Elephant Hill proves too steep. Amy and I take
it easy around camp, do schoolwork, and read. Amy bakes a cherry cobbler.
Mmm, it's good.

After two days at Canyonlands, we drive on. It snows on us a bit coming down Interstate 70 into Salina, but we head for Maple Grove, where we
have stayed before. While Nate and Amy keep warm by hitting the badminton birdie back and forth, Don takes me for a walk. Away from the trees,
the slope fans out below our hillside oasis. I pause to make a quick sketch.
The rounded tops of sage and other shrubs remind me of eroded sandstone
and newly forming cumulus clouds. This artist is having a pattern review.

We walk the trail to the base of the mountain and discover what drew
the Mormon pioneers here in the first place: water gushes from under the
rock. It's a spring of biblical proportions and flows with a steady stream of
life-giving water. An image surfaces in my mind: an old picture of Moses

striking the rock to get water in the wilderness.[1] What a gift to find water in a thirsty land. Water is life in the desert. And "living water," what's that all about?

> DON: *November. It's getting late in the season, but we drive on to Zion and spend three nights. Lots of spaces in the campground. Cottonwoods are prime color and leaves are falling, blowing everywhere. We drive the canyon and hike several places. Lots to photograph.*
>
> *In camp, Nate finds a Desert Spiny Lizard on a branch next to our picnic table. Looks like a small prehistoric monster with its hackles up. It's a good tree climber. Nate is afraid he will get bit if he picks it up. I grab it behind the head and hold on tight. It's a monster all right and would cheerfully take a chunk out of my hand.*

We are all a little homesick, but here we are at Zion. We wanted to see it in the off-season. It's warm in the canyon and a good day for painting. After Nate and Amy finish their daily math assignment, we drive to the end of the paved road. The family deposits me creekside between towering cliff walls. They go up the trail toward the Narrows. I step on stones and gravel bars to cross the creek—well, a river actually, the Virgin River in its beginning journey. I park my gear between clumps of willow and set up my art stool in the shade of a big cottonwood. I pull out paints and look around. Sunshine washes the sandstone canyon walls with myriad shades of earth colors—coral, pink, orange, and yellow ochre. The air glows golden in the radiant light, even yellowing the shadows where I sit.

I paint and sketch for a long while: the creek, the willows, the cottonwood, the base of the cliff near me. The longer I sit, the more content I become. A great peace floods through me. I stop working and listen to the quiet, attending to the murmuring stream and occasional birdcalls. Another beautiful moment.

One epiphany after another has been the unexpected bonus to my journey so far. Just being here, looking, listening, touching, and inhaling the fragrant earth, air, and vegetation seems to be the catalyst for these special moments. Does God have anything to do with it? That thought is still very tender. I have questions. Some folks say it's all science, that the universe just happened. I wonder if they have ever been out in the field like this, living with nature, breathing truly fresh air, observing the ways of

---

1. Exod 17:6–7: "I will stand there before you by the rock at Horeb. Strike the rock, and water will come out of it for the people to drink" (NIV). So Moses did this in the sight of the elders of Israel.

water, at times battling the elements, seeing and hearing what it's really like. After the holidays, we will take up our journey again. The pilgrimage is not yet over. I seek more evidence. That's the rational thing to do.

Dwarfed by canyon walls of monumental and glorious design, I am roused by my inner art instructor, who says: Let's take another look. Nuances of light find hidden cracks and crevices in the rock as the sun slowly arcs toward the western rim. Colors change as new contours are highlighted. It is like a Master Painter wielding the expressive tools that every artist strives to employ, including shading, intensity, value, tone, and movement. Emotional impact flows from the differences in light and shadow, color tints and shades, textures, varied lines and shapes, contoured forms, and the creative use of space. I can even point out the use of contrast, dominance, and emphasis—the expressive principles of art. Right in this canyon, I am living an art appreciation course that ranks with the best.

This canyon design is not a product of rigid formula. John Ruskin, the nineteenth-century English art critic, advised that "some irregularity in a noble composition benefits the unity, the overall effect."[2] Here nothing is truly perfect in the sandstone, cloudless sky, trees, murmuring stream, birdsong, and the human souls that are present, but each is different, each contributes to unity. As Ruskin might observe, all are in harmonious service to the whole artwork. That's a good rule for an ecosystem too. I wish Ruskin could have seen Zion Canyon.

All this sounds too intellectual for this warm, sunny place. Even though theory is demonstrated in practice, I close my eyes and take a deep breath. I can hold such beauty only in small doses, and I long to hang on to the moment. The stones reflect warmth from the sun. Fluttering leaves whisper small truths. Something nudges me. I can only describe it as a spirit of painting. It fills the canyon and wraps around my heart. It calls to my inner artist in a message for all painters: *Come, be a witness. The beauty is here to share.*

> DON: *Drive west to Lehman Caves. We reach Lehman Creek and feel like we are almost home. Cold here. Late fall look to everything. Aspen leaves are gone, but trunks blaze white in the sun and show off black scars of age. Undergrowth of wild roses are brilliant red with orange rosehips.*

---

2. Ruskin, *Elements of Drawing*, 133. Art critic Ruskin was also draughtsman, watercolorist, prominent social thinker, and philanthropist. Today, his ideas and concerns are widely recognized as having anticipated environmentalism, sustainability, and craft.

We pull into our favorite campsite and stare. Nature's art gallery is aflame with one final going-home display. It's November already, so the colors are late, unexpected, and intense. By the creek, the wild roses are a tangle of scarlet and coral leaves, maroon stems, and bright orange rose-hips. That wild palette is set against the black-and-white aspen trunks with their branches bared to the elements. Don digs out his camera. I dive for my art pack. What a stunning finish to this part of our trip. We won't forget. We'll be back.

Great are the works of the LORD;
they are pondered by all who delight in them.

—Ps 111:2–4, NIV

PART II

The most beautiful thing we can experience is the mysterious.
It is the source of all true art and science.

—ALBERT EINSTEIN[1]

O God, what mysteries I find in thee! How vast the number of thy purposes!
I try to count them?—they are more than the sand;
I wake from my reverie, and I am still lost in thee.

—Ps 139:17–18, MOFFATT

1. Einstein, *Hand of God*, 37.

Arrowweed, Death Valley, , California

13

Southwest, California
Death Valley National Park

On the road again, dust storm, and rain shadows

It's been good to be home for the holidays, and I confess my misgivings about trying to camp and live in the trailer during the short, dark days of winter. Cabin fever can happen even in a trailer, especially with two energetic children. While we're home, our renter friends have been kind enough to allow the children back into their bedrooms. They both returned to school for this short time. Don and I are making do with the home studio space, and we cook and sleep in the trailer.

As departure time draws near, we assess gear and necessities for camping. Don draws up a list of wild edible plants found in the Southwest so he can photograph them. We live too far away for casual camera treks into the deserts of the Southwest. For most of the plants, we check the herbariums at the parks, where the rangers are always helpful. Specimens are labeled with locations, and we can then search for them in the field. For the more obscure plants, Don now has a New Mexico contact who knows plants and where to find them. In no time at all, we are ready to get back on the road, but we wait. It is storming in the mountains.

DON: *March 1. Departure delayed two weeks due to too much mountain snow for the trailer. Weather finally clears, and we take off. Snowbanks along the road are not very deep because of drought. Road is dry, and that's all we need.*

A break in the weather is just what we've been waiting for. We pile into the rig and drive over the mountains. We roll south through a wintry Nevada—no snow, just dormant plant life and cold. We stop overnight in Tonopah, elevation 6000 feet. The temperature drops to five degrees, and our outside trailer pipe freezes solid, which is not a good start to our next odyssey. Pouring hot water over the pipe is a lesson in futility. I hunt down the hot water bottle, fill it from a heated teakettle, and lay it on top of the pipe. After a while, it works. The ice melts. We fill up with water, clear our disposal tanks, and then are off to Death Valley.

Since Tonopah, the children ride in Aunt Nancy's car; they are pretty sure she will stop for ice cream cones. Nancy is doing fieldwork in the area for the U.S. Geological Survey. Everywhere we stop, she and Don botanize, identifying unknown plants. She is looking for plants that indicate minerals in the soil in areas pinpointed by remote sensing imagery. What a contrast to Gold Rush days, when old time prospectors walked every inch of this ground with a burro, gold pan, canteen, and a sack of grub. They didn't stop to botanize.

AMY: *Dear Diary,*

Today we are in Death Valley. I flew my kite, "the eagle," way up high. I like this place. Aunt Nancy and Dad went looking for plants. I stayed home. I also did some of my schoolwork. P.S. My class gave me a goodbye party when I left. I miss everyone at home.

The drive opens new vistas of desert as we turn toward Death Valley itself. The bones of the earth are visible here, with the earth stripped bare. My drawing hand itches for pen and sketchbook. I love drawing landforms, erosion patterns, cliffs, and drainages. Park Service signs tell us how it works: the mountain is the source, while the erosional plane is called the pediment. The resultant sand and gravel wash downhill to land on the *bajada*, the depositional plain, also called the alluvial fan. It's a different language. My inner artist doesn't think in geological terms. I think in images.

Spring flowers dot the alluvial fans. In one area, Desert Gold blooms as far as we can see, each wildflower positioned a certain distance from the next in a natural distribution. We find early desert mariposa, gravel ghost, and clusters of desert five-spot, each delicate white cup marked with five maroon spots. Rainfall was moderate last fall and did not trigger an abundance of blooms this spring, but we are satisfied.

AMY: *Dear Diary,*

I have a tree to climb right in our campsite. It is great. Grandma and Grandpa are here. Nate and I got to stay one night at the motel and swim in the pool. Grandma helped me finish my nine-patch doll quilt I made for the Centennial. Tonight I have to wash dishes. I hate it.

Every day we drive to a different area in this huge park. Badwater Basin salt flats cover an expanse of two hundred square miles. Blindingly white in the sun, it's like an enormous geometric puzzle on dazzling display. I sit in the shade of the pickup truck to draw while the others explore with the visiting grandparents. They call me over to see a small salt pool. Salt crystals float on the surface like clusters of little ice flowers in circular pattern. This is a radial arrangement, a mix of the different mineral salts found in this location—probably calcite, gypsum, and borax. We watch as one salt cluster grows too heavy to float and gently sinks to the bottom of the pool. The clear water is an odd shade of blue with brown. The perimeter of the pool is crusty with the salt deposits. Common table salt normally crystalizes into little cubes with flat faces. The salt atoms assemble in such an orderly way that Don says we can cleave a table salt crystal with a razor blade and get more cubes. Amazing. When I get back to camp, I'm going to get out the saltshaker and a magnifying glass.

Don sets up the big telephoto lens to get a close-up of the crystals. I go back to drawing. The snow-covered Panamint Mountains rise more than 11,000 feet to the west. What a contrast to this basin, the lowest spot in the western hemisphere. We are 282 feet below sea level.

From the lowest spot, we drive up to Dantes View and look down on the salt flats over 5000 feet below. An ocean of white, the salt deposits lie in undulating patterns like frozen foam on a motionless sea. I see repeated forms, familiar lines, structural wonders, all in the simplicity of basic patterns. It's yet another witness to creative unity! What a grand scheme— from the smallest crystal to this sweeping vista, the art principles apply. The scope is hard to grasp.

DON: *Not much growing in the valley. Too many minerals. This is Mojave Desert. Creosote bush is not far away, also yucca, agave, rabbitbrush, sage, and Joshua Trees on the foothills. Rangers still discover new species. I get permission to photograph the Rock Lady*

*near Titus Canyon because of my college permits. We four-wheel
down Titus Canyon. The Rock Ladies are only five in number, below
recovery level, although more may be found elsewhere. The blooming plants hang upside down in a hollowed-out cave. How can they
possibly reproduce like that? Another ranger stops by while I am
photographing. He accepts my explanation. Very friendly.*

We finally take the drive along the Artist's Palette road. That is not an overstatement. The earth tones are vibrant and varied: reds, grays, blacks, browns, whites, ochres, and greens color the rock. If there is any blue rock, I miss it. This is a popular road, so there's lots of traffic. Even so, I wish we had come here sooner. Now there's not enough time to do it justice. We must come back.

Our friends the Livingstons arrive from Oregon to camp with us for a few days. Nate and Duncan hunt golf balls in the ditch by the golf range close to camp. They hoard them like treasure. We walk the nearby date grove and pick up a few dry, wrinkled things that have fallen off the trees. It's hard to believe they make succulent morsels.

A light breeze kicks up on the morning the crew starts out for Titus Canyon. Since we drove that canyon last week, I opt for a solitary day in camp. My stroll around the campground is cut short by small gusts of wind that scatter sand across the path. Back in the trailer, I close windows. Before long, dust blows everywhere, and I can't see past the smoke trees across the way. The wind grows stronger and hurls sand at anyone bold enough to go out. I hope Titus Canyon is not windy.

From the safety of the trailer, I watch the dust storm build. This could get mean. A strong gust buffets the trailer, and dust sifts down over the table. I blow off my sketchbook and put it away. I forgot to tighten the roof vents. Outside, the wind sweeps away branches, leaves, and camp debris. I watch it tumble across the campground. Murky air obscures camp tables and vehicles. An upended dome tent rolls past, which is ludicrous to watch but probably not so funny to the absent owners. Two or three upright aluminum pie plates roll merrily along, accompanied by a flying tablecloth and newspapers. I have a ringside seat for the show, but it is sobering. Raw power drives this dust storm; the elements are at work.

To keep my mind busy I pull out some hand sewing and embroider a few of those desert gold wildflowers onto my own quilt project. About three hours later, the wind lessens, and the family truck emerges out of the dust cloud. Thankfully, the storm was not a problem in Titus Canyon, but they did run into it when they reached the highway.

The wind gradually blows itself away. I heave a sigh of relief. Inside the trailer, a fine dust has settled on flat surfaces and collected under doorsills. Our shade tree lost a few small branches, but otherwise we have no damage. What really impresses the boys, however, is the campground outhouse. It blew over and now lays on its side.

> Don: *We eat supper at Stovepipe Wells. Old-timers dug wells here, then shoved in a stovepipe to keep the sandy sides from caving in. Scoured by wind, flooded by rain, and baked in the sun, the desert floor takes a beating. Even so, we find reeds and willows around water sources, including the seep willow, but we see no native palm trees. Not easy for plants to survive here, but some specialized plants are found nowhere else. The water back at camp is amazingly good. It comes from springs up the canyon.*

In the evening, we light a small campfire and talk over the day's adventures. After the fire burns out, everyone else heads for bed, but I grab my flashlight. I watch for snakes as Don and I walk out into the desert beyond the campground. I switch off the light. Pitch blackness wraps around us like a cloak. Overhead, a star dance is going on. "Look at the stars! Look, look up at the skies! O look at all the fire-folk sitting in the air!"[1] The old poem rings in my memory. Glittering sparks of light shift and wink when I try to focus on one. I scan the Milky Way that pours across the sky. This is the darkest of dark nights we have encountered. Not really black, it must be Payne's gray or indigo, or maybe it's just deep navy color—I can't decide. We are spellbound, quiet, holding to heart the wonder of such a sight after the dust-stormy day. This is what we seek. No, that's not quite right. This is *where* we seek. I stare farther and farther into the midnight dark space, looking deeper. My inner artist reaches out, wanting to go there, to search the dark mystery, and to find what must exist beyond that deep dark, the light that overcomes darkness.

Gradually, the nighttime chill penetrates the bones. I look about. The night is not as dark as I thought. Starlight shows the path, and we walk back to camp in silence.

Much of Death Valley lies between two mountain ranges in a double rain shadow. Rains from the west seldom make it over the mountains, nor do rains from the east. When it does rain, the runoff floods down bare

---

1. Hopkins, "Starlight Night," 128.

slopes into the valley and forms a lake that has no outlet. The lake evaporates seasonally and leaves mineral salt deposits, which are not conducive to life.

Physical events shape, mold, build up, and tear down the bare bones of existence, yet Death Valley is anything but dead. Despite the stark environment, extremes in temperatures, elevations, winds, water cycles that offer floods on one hand and complete drought on the other, dust storms, and relentless sun—despite all that—life does survive. Living conditions may be harsh, but area plants and animals are highly adapted for survival. Here is a lesson in barebones living, paring down nonessentials to utilize the essential. It's economy again, an art lesson for life.

> DON: *I could spend another month here photographing. We must move south though, or we are going to miss spring flowers in the Sonoran Desert. Tomorrow, we head for Organ Pipe.*

I ponder the lessons of Death Valley as we drive south into the Sonoran Desert. More epiphanies and more heart-stopping moments shape our journey. Last summer and fall our adventures awakened every sense. As a teacher, I know the first step in learning is sensation, then awareness, then perception, and finally cognition. Daily, the whole family grows more aware. We notice more, then compare and enjoy it as we explore further. Love for the land seeps into our days as travel literally expands our horizons. Even the children revel in the elements. I'm back to art basics here: mass, space, and light.

My family and I dare to live close to the earth for this limited time. What a gift. We seek adventure and want to study. Each experience hold primary truths about the elements of the earth, the processes that govern life communities, and the interrelationships that make life possible. Who can argue with such a grounded reality? Living close to the elements, close to the earth, has brought us recognition of the vital energy of all living things. Sensing the spiritual energy is part of the mix. Is this the sixth sense at work? Energy by itself is an active force, but it is not the source. Where does it come from? What is the ultimate source?

Arizona landscape rolls past as we drive. Comparisons abound. Land contours and shapes change from the flowing lines of the Great Basin of Nevada and Utah. A different geology molds the foothills, which appear lumpy and stark. Desert plants are also lumpy and stark, especially the cactus. Even the colors are changing. I hope I have the right ones in my art pack.

If I say, "The dark will screen me, night will hide me in its curtains."
Yet darkness is not dark to thee, the night is clear as daylight.

—PS 139:11–12, MOFFATT

Lost Dutchman State Park, Superstition Mountains, Arizona

14

Southwest, Arizona

*Organ Pipe National Monument,
Tubac, and Tucson.*

Transition time, sketching cactus, and a real artist

DON: *April. Head south to Organ Pipe. Sonoran Desert is a whole
new world to us northerners. Rough country, sparse vegetation, forbidding landscape, cacti armed and ready. Yet the desert is healthy,
not dying. It's robust with life—desert life.*

I lean out the trailer door to see what's keeping Don. Murmurs and
laughter erupt from the pup tent. I look up at the night sky and catch my
breath. The moon is in eclipse! The bold crescent dominates the desert sky,
with the shadowed side a sphere of odd light that is dimly coral in color.
I call to the family, but after a brief three-person looksee out the tent flap,
Don's storytelling continues.

Keeping an eye out for visiting rattlesnakes, I walk to the edge of the
pavement. Cactus silhouettes and shadowed shapes blend into the desert
dark. This is Organ Pipe Cactus National Monument, a reserve that holds
Arizona's stand of unique cactus. To the north, the upper Sonoran Desert is
home to saguaro cactus. Here, in the monument, we find a mix of saguaros
and organ pipe cactus. Saguaro growth ends at this point, but organ pipe

cactus spreads south into Mexico. It's all connected, all related, but vegetation patterns shift. This area between upper and lower Sonoran Desert is a transition area. There's that metaphor again. It's like this yearlong camping trip. I could get philosophical, but not now. Tonight, philosophy takes a backseat. Tonight, it's all sky mystery, night poetry.

I watch the slow progression of shadow over the moon. A breath of wind rustles creosote bushes. Something whirrs past my head, barely discernible in the dark against dark. Was that a bat? If it was a bat, it's early. The organ pipe cacti aren't blooming for another month. When the bloom occurs, nectar-eating bats will flock into this area. They migrate from Central Mexico and follow the cacti bloom season. The "nectar trail" leads here. Organ pipe and saguaro bloom at night and provide nectar for the bats. The bats pollinate the flowers in turn—a vital relationship in the endless network.

Moon and shadow hold center stage. A faint flutter of stars wink in the afterglow. Wonder seizes my heart and clings to memory. I wish we could do this all the time. So does Don. Even surrounded by this rough and formidable landscape, the land lies around us like an open book, revealing life and what it holds.

We tend to disregard what it takes to make this trip because the wonders are so unforgettable. The required work, planning, and expenses are a given. It's worth it, so we downplay car trouble, flat tires, noisy neighbors, barking dogs, illness, threatening weather, and even the rattlesnakes we have been warned about. Rattlesnakes are nocturnal and like to bask on pavement still warm from the sun. I carry my flashlight just in case.

None of life's problems detract from the freedom we have. They don't spoil our expanded sense of space and landscape. Neither cost nor risk can mask the renewal of spiritual connection. As a child, I learned about God. As a teen, my understanding was corrupted by the negative and legalistic teaching of a self-appointed church patriarch. That bitter memory is fading. The peace and love I find outdoors stirs teachings long forgotten: God is love, God is close and personal, God is in charge. A myth? Some say so, but my perception is changing.

AMY: *Dear Diary,*

We went to Quitobaquito Springs. When we got there, we walked around the pond. Mom and I saw a phainopepla with a crest on its head. It was black. There also was a big cottonwood leaning over the water. Nate and I climbed all over it. While we were on the tree,

there were softshell turtles below us, wild ones. In a little while, we
ate lunch and Mom and I saw an oriole. Then we stepped under the
fence into Mexico.

Amy and I spot our first cardinal, bright red, perching in the willows. Nonmigratory, it prefers to stay year-round in the Southwest. However, a primary migratory bird flyway does pass through this area, and this pond is an important oasis. I listen to birdsong as I sketch the cottonwood across the pond. I still experiment with media, and today I'm trying pastels. My technique is elementary, but the pastels flow easily onto the paper. They don't travel well though, which is a requirement for this trip. Constant motion smears the colors even when I protect the pages. Before long, I may give them up. They are fun to experiment with, but they are not quite my style.

I squint at the pond for colors and flowing lines, yet I begin to see a very different picture. I close my eyes. My inner picture is of a small pool of quiet water below a rock crevice. The rocks are sandstone, in earth colors of red, coral, and yellow ochre. Green algae grows in the shallows, where the sandstone and blue sky are reflected in the water. I store the image in my mental gallery for later. I love the color combinations. It seems to me that certain colors in nature are often grouped together. Can I call them natural combinations? Can I log them just like the flowing line patterns I have found? This particular combination of colors fascinates me—earth red and algae green combined with dried grass colors. Hmm. Patterns of color? That's something to watch for.

The children climb onto the big cottonwood branch that reaches out over the pond. Nate wants to take home one of the softshell turtles; Amy prefers a baby cactus. I envision living four months with a turtle and a kissing cactus, and I give it a thumbs down. At any rate, desert life is protected here—that's what the park is all about. These wonderful creatures need their own home. Aha! Out from behind a desert shrub comes a roadrunner! And there he goes, running toward the border fence. I love roadrunners. My day is now complete.

Don comes around the other side of the pond carrying his tripod and big lens. He scares up a new bird in the willows—a flash of black, white, and orange—an oriole. Another new bird for my beginner's bird list. Such simple things bring such pleasure. We eat lunch at the picnic table and then crawl under the fence to step into Mexico before we go back to camp. The days are rapidly getting warmer. We may head north soon.

DON: *Stop for a Gila monster along the road to Quitobaquito. It crawls away up a small wash in the sand. Lots of bird life around the springs. Water tastes surprisingly good. Spot a phainopepla. I've never seen one before. Curve-billed thrasher, cactus wren, and the Gila woodpecker are in the neighborhood, and the common raven also. Wildflowers on the wane, but we find patches here and there of Mexican poppies, lupine, owl clover, and globemallow. The nature trail helped to identify shrubs such as creosote, brittlebush, and of course the cactus, saguaro, organ pipe, pincushion, and cholla. Nate and I will take the ranger-led nature walk. Evening programs at the campground are great.*

Back in camp, I commandeer the camper. I clear one bunk and set out my large paper and board. Small color studies are good for color choices and rough sketches, but they don't satisfy. It's time to work larger. The picture I envisioned earlier takes shape with preliminary sketches. Even though I don't recall actually seeing this spring anywhere on our hikes, I have a clear idea of what it looks like. An intuitive painting? Must be. I prepare larger pans of watercolor so I can use larger brushes. I fill the clean water can and the washup water can and begin. Later, when I show the finished picture to Don and Nate, they say it looks like a spring they saw on their nature hike. Hmm. I can't explain it.

We drive north toward Tucson. Patches of yellow dot the desert. It's some kind of poppy we think. We are late for most spring flowers, which shows our inexperience with the low desert. Next trip to the Sonoran Desert, we'll try to come in March and monitor the weather patterns more closely.

DON: *Geologically, we are no longer in the Great Basin, but we are still within the Basin and Range Province. Like Nevada and southeastern Oregon, fault block ranges rise out of broad Sonoran valleys. Lava rock is exposed in some areas as a relic of a bygone era of volcanic activity. Prickly pear cacti abound along with agaves, mesquite, and catclaw accacia.*

At every turn, we fall under the spell of the Southwest even more: adobe homes hung with strings of drying red peppers, stucco walls with blue doors, agaves everywhere, prickly pear, a cactus landscape, saguaro sentinels, ocotillo in bloom, mountain vistas on the horizon, and sweeping valleys with spinning dust devils. Ancient and modern Indian culture mixes with Spanish influence and combines with modern-day America, a cultural extravaganza.

We arrive at Tucson's Arizona-Sonora Desert Museum. Part zoo and part botanical garden, we can study native plants and live animals here in their native habitats. Arizona plant communities are still foreign to us. We want to connect names with actual faces.

Don carries his big lens and tripod down the sandy path and sets up by the desert tortoise compound. I walk around for a bit until I find a cactus garden that is native to Arizona. I set down my stool, adjust my hat brim, and begin to draw. Spherical cactus shapes are almost pure form. The primary outlines are cone, sphere, and cylinder, familiar student subject matter. I decide to treat cactus like a still life. To start with, I ignore spines and sketch the underlying shape. My inner instructor asks: Is it a sphere, egg shape, barrel shape, pear shape, or column? Are the parallel ribs all vertical, or do they spiral around the shape? I look for patterns, even double patterns. How do arms project from the main body? Observe the joint area: Is the angle up, down, or straight? How does the plant cover the joint? Count the raised areas, or aureoles. Plot them on paper to establish the pattern. Do spines or tufts appear on the aureoles? How many spines? Are the tufts all mature, or do they range from immature to mature spines along the spiral pattern? Are the spines straight or hooked? Are there minute hairs or total smoothness? I shade rounded shapes just like I did in Drawing 101, first observing the direction of the light source, then adding textural details. It works.

The pencil drawings turn out well. I'll ink them later. Right now, the sun is gaining strength. I pick up my art stool and head for shade and a cool drink. As I sit in the Ramada area, two Mexican children with dark hair and dark eyes burst out the museum door and run past me. I admire their beautiful coloring and special grace. When two mothers follow, they smile at me while watching their children, then turn toward blonde, fair-skinned, blue-eyed Amy, who is coming my way. What a contrast. We laugh because we so admire each other's children.

> DON: *Desert Museum is a great place for close-up animal photography. I set up cameras by the prairie dog compound and get lots of shots. Move on to bighorn sheep, who seem to pose. The coyotes are restless and won't hold still for long. The javelina get up and crawl into the brush, then lay down with huge sighs and snorts. The keeper throws them watermelon and they come out to eat it. I can't photograph them eating watermelon. It needs to be wild food. Black vulture sits on a branch—a different species than we have at home.*

White-winged doves flutter around. This species is special to the south desert.

From miles away, we can see the "white dove of the desert," San Xavier del Bac. The eighteenth-century cathedral stands alone, white and imposing in the dry brown landscape south of Tucson. We pull into the dust-blown parking area and pile out of the truck. Outside the ornately carved entrance, we stop to buy Indian fry bread that is hot, crispy, and sweet with sugar. Two Papago Indian women smile and nod as they serve us from their stand.

The sculpted facade and white towers loom above us in the Arizona sun. We step into the dim cathedral, momentarily blinded, and we sense the hush that has fallen on tourists and local folk alike. Some wander the aisles, and others sit quietly in the old wooden pews. High along the side walls, statues of saints look down upon us from their niches. Faded paintings and scrollwork cover the lofty ceiling and plaster surfaces. Everything looks old, old, old. Paint is chipped and plaster cracked here and there, but some woodwork is covered with burnished gold leaf that still glows in the dim light.

I rest for a few moments in one of the straight-backed old pews. I imagine all the prayers that have been lifted up in this sanctuary since the 1700s. I close my eyes and sense the same peace I have encountered in outdoor sanctuaries. The walls seem alive with whispers like the sound of fluttering aspen leaves—whispers of praise. I add a few of my own.

The mission was founded in 1692 by Father Eusebio Kino, a Jesuit missionary and explorer of the Southwest and northern Mexico. The current cathedral was started in 1783 and completed in 1797. It still retains the original purpose as a mission to local people. We wander through the enclave, out into the desert garden, and through old halls and walkways to the gift shop before doubling back to the sanctuary. Serenity reigns.

As we leave, a couple of musicians with violin cases tucked under their arms stroll past us through the front door. I turn back and follow them into the sanctuary. Music stands and chairs are being placed down front. I want to stay. The children are restless, but the family sits with me for a while. Stringed instruments are tuned for rehearsal as members of the Tucson Symphony prepare an Easter celebration. They lift their bows, and the pure, almost elemental sound of strings rises into sacred space. It fills the ancient hall and reverberates off high ceilings. Melodies rise and fall, sweetly sonorous, yet joyful for the Easter season. One by one, the rest of the family slips away, but I close my eyes, enchanted with the lines of melody that double back in echo to mix into a blend of woven harmonies and trailing phrases that resound wondrously in that high vault.

I stay as long as I dare, then quietly withdraw to join the others. I promised the children we would decorate Easter eggs back at the trailer, and Amy has a sewing project to finish. All the way back to camp, I still hear music. Easter joy sings in my head.

> DON: *We drive south to Tubac, exploring the area. Diverse life forms survive here. A fascinating variety of plants and animals have adapted to harsh growing conditions. Life itself is the miracle.*

We enter an art gallery in Tubac, and a moment later, in walks the artist, Hugh Cabot. I'm already admiring his oil painting *Cibolla*, which hangs on the wall—an ominous evening storm bears down on an adobe building that glows red and coral from low sunlight. Strong juicy colors are broadly brushed to heighten the abstract qualities of a recognizable desert landscape. I would gladly take it home with me. We strike up a conversation with Hugh Cabot and his wife, who runs the gallery. We talk for over an hour about wild edible plants, about our year of camping, about Southern Arizona. When he finds out I'm the illustrator of the plant book and learning watercolor, he starts to talk about painting. I listen carefully to tips about how he works, his favorite sketching pen, his system for transporting drawing materials, the need for discipline, and his father's advice: "Do what you believe in or you'll never amount to anything." He finishes by pulling a framed ink sketch off the wall and handing it to us. "Send me one of your books," he says.

When we get back to Tucson, we go right to a bookstore and find our *Wild Edible Plants* book on the shelf. Don buys the new color copy. The next morning, we drive back down to Tubac and give Hugh the book. He is surprised and pleased.

Later, I locate an office supply store and buy the exact pens he recommended. I like the pens, and they are filled with permanent ink. I reorganize my own sketching setup and try his travel system. Every time I look at the desert sky, I hear him say, "The color of the overhead western sky is thalo blue." I plan to pick up a tube and try it.

❧

See, I am doing a new thing! Now it springs up; do you not perceive it?
I am making a way in the desert.

—ISA 43:19, NIV

Pasqueflower, Haviland Lake, San Juan Mountains, Colorado

15

Southwest, Arizona

Traveling North, Roosevelt Dam,
and Colorado Mountains.

Desert farewell, troublemakers, and small graces

Don: *Desert heat sends us north too soon. Must come back. The biota is fascinating. Enjoyed the Phoenix Botanical Garden, Phoenix Zoo, and the Heard Museum, where Nate talked us into buying two Kachinas. Stopped at Boyce Thompson Arboretum east of Phoenix. Just what we needed: desert plant communities in natural surroundings. Jan heard cañon wrens one more time and sketched a lot. We now head for Petrified Forest National Park.*

"No Trailers Beyond This Point." Just as we zoom past, I catch a glimpse of the battered and dusty old sign. It leans toward the lake and points aimlessly at the sky. Too late, the road is already dropping down to the dam, and there's no place to turn around.

"It's on the map," declares Don in a firm voice. "This is the road."

Below us, a one-lane passage traces the graceful curve of the Roosevelt Dam. Ready or not, we are driving across the dam, trailer and all. The narrow crossway begins and ends with a sharp right-angle turn. How did we get into this? No early warning. I can't look.

Feeling silly and out of place, we make the first sharp turn. A worker pickup pulls into the inner space of the angle so we can get by. We barely fit wall-to-wall as we cross the dam with a half-filled lake on one side and the deep gorge of the Salt River on the other. Two cars wait for us on the other side of the dam. They grin and wave as we sail past. Embarrassing, but we made it. The rubble-masonry dam is still intact, grand, and noble. All is serene. We pull over and park so we can take a look. A national historic landmark, the dam was completed in 1911 and dedicated by Theodore Roosevelt. For a time, it was the tallest masonry dam in the world and held back the largest artificial lake, Theodore Roosevelt Lake. A showpiece of craftsmanship, this huge dam looks handmade.[1]

We drive on to the campground at the north end of the lake. Several boats are out on the water. The area is dry from drought, but after a month in the low desert, I'm glad to see pine trees. I remind Nate to bring his journal up to date while Amy and I go for a walk. Down by the water, we pass a stand of willows. A flash of pure blue disappears into the leafy shrubbery. What's that? We stand still. The bluest bird I've ever seen flits to a nearby branch. We are spellbound. Back at the trailer, we look it up in the bird book—a mountain bluebird, what a beauty!

We drive north to the Painted Desert and Petrified Forest. We overnight in Holbrook and then spend a day driving the park roads. Geology is an open book here, with sunrise colors painted on the badlands. I marvel that eons ago, a lush forest grew in this place, and the trees are still here, fossilized as stone.

> DON: *Vegetation is sparse; bare soils and bedrock are exposed. I spot a juniper or two and some shrubs, but mostly grasses have taken hold here. Wildflower season is early yet. We find Indian paintbrush and early globemallow. Colorful lichens are common on the rocks.*
>
> *Photograph the petrified wood. The detail in the agatized wood is very colorful, with clearly outlined tree rings. The crystal formations fracture so cleanly that many logs look like they were sawed in two. I crouch down in the dirt to focus on a fossilized stump; I glance up to see a green collared lizard watching me over the top of the stump. When I move, he jumps off the stump, stands on his back legs, and takes off running. Hilarious to watch. Nate chases him but can't catch him.*

1. In 1999, extensive renovation changed the design and materials of the dam, and the National Historic Landmark designation was withdrawn. As part of the renovation a much-needed automotive bridge was constructed from one side of the lake to the other.

Two days later, we drive into Durango. We are glad to be back in Colorado's mountains. After a day of rest and laundry at the United Camp Ground, we restock groceries, including cake mix and birthday candles. Two birthdays are coming up soon. Don buys fishing worms, and we head for Haviland Lake. The lake is full to the brim, and my fisherfolk are itching to try their luck.

We set up camp close to the lakeshore. Except for weekend fishermen, this camp is mostly deserted at this time of year, and the place seems lonely. We chat with the ranger who drives through, but otherwise we are by ourselves the first night. I am uneasy.

The next morning dawns bright and sunny, and the crew pulls the boat off the trailer and carries it over to the water. Fish are biting, and the three fishermen happily row around until Amy's pole breaks. They let her off on the bank, and she traipses back into camp, where I am sketching with my new Hugh Cabot-style clipboard and cardstock. The Pentel pens are juicy with permanent ink. The flow is effortless, and so far no leaks and no messes.

Across the lake, the Hermosa Cliffs rise out of forested slopes. I love to sketch cliffs and slopes where trees line the ravines and spread down to the great forests of ponderosa and aspen. When I stand up, however, I'm horrified. My jeans are crawling with ticks. I stamp my feet and brush off as many as I can. I head for the trailer to change clothes and dispose of stragglers. Ugh. Paradise is not so perfect after all. Range cattle, deer, and elk roam through here, all tick carriers, and I have seen my share, but this is the worst I've ever experienced.

AMY: *Dear Diary,*

Today is Dad's birthday. He is forty-two. I gave him a fish pillow I sewed. We had cake and ice cream.

Today is overcast and cool. The fishermen take the boat to the other side of the lake, just out of sight of the trailer. I am indoors reading when an old pickup drives by very slowly. The driver looks us over and sees me inside. He's no camper, that's for sure, and he drives on past. I make sure the doors and windows are locked. A few minutes later, he comes back and parks nearby. He stands outside in scruffy brown hat and shapeless coat and hollers at me through the closed window, asking directions. I shake my head and gesture ignorance, but I don't go near the door. After he walks back and forth a bit, he climbs into the truck and drives off. I don't like it. I don't feel safe.

I wait over half an hour. I wonder if Don and the children are coming back yet. I finally calm down, but I'm restless. I decide to walk around the lakeshore; maybe I can see the boat. I make it down to the lake, and hurray! They are in view, rowing in my direction. I look back. The pickup has returned, this time with two disreputable-looking men and a dog. The first fellow hustles in my direction, gesturing to the dog. He's between me and the trailer and appears threatening. His friend waits by the truck. The dog is coming my way when the boat reaches shore. Don leaps out and leaves Nate to handle the boat. Don barrels up from the beach and heads right for the troublemaker, hollering a warning to him to get out of here. In short order, the two men and dog jump in their truck and speed away. That was quite a scare.

We report the incident to the ranger, but I'm still uneasy the next day. We have had so little trouble on this trip, but we are always careful: we keep daylight hours, stay together, and camp in what appear to be safe places. Don and I talk about the incident as we walk up the hill by the lake. This morning, spring is in the air, and the leafless aspen shine with catkins. Dry pine needles crunch underfoot, making the hill a bit slippery. We've been here a week already, but now we no longer feel safe by ourselves. It's time to move on.

A little farther on, we are surprised to find clumps of delicate, pale lavender flowers that have thrust up from the thick carpet of dry, brown pine needles. I go down on my knees to get a closer look. The size and growth pattern remind me of spring crocus, but these flowers have six graceful petals that form a cup that holds a cluster of yellow stamens. It's a reward for early season naturalists like us. Don says the petals are not true petals but sepals colored pale lavender. Both stems and sepals are covered with delicate hairs, which give them an ethereal appearance in the sunlight like all-over halos. I pull out my sketchbook. Don pulls out the flower book. New to us, these are pasqueflower (*Anemone patens L.*), which are evidently common in many areas. "Pasque" refers to Easter; *Anemone* means "wind flower." We are surrounded by Easter wind flowers.

At the first hint of the breeze that springs up, the delicate blossoms begin to bend. The wind ripples on down the slope, and the silky flowers serve as nature's indicator of which way the wind is blowing. I sit back on my heels and shift my vision into drawing and painting mode. All becomes poetry in the morning light—catkin halos, Easter flowers, ethereal wind dancers, all are great scope for the imagination.[2] And what would we do without imagination? It expands the imagery to fuel poetry and the arts. It's required for creativity, invention, and problem-solving of all sorts.

I attempt a pen sketch, but my lines are too bold, too numerous to capture the delicacy of the pasqueflowers. I can't yet do justice to the wonders of nature. It's in the details, and the details add up. I'm beginning to agree with Albert Einstein, who said: "My religion consists of a humble admiration of the illimitable superior spirit who reveals himself in the slight details we are able to perceive with our frail and feeble minds. That deeply emotional conviction of the presence of a superior reasoning power, which is revealed in the incomprehensible universe, forms my idea of God."[3]

> AMY: *We stayed seven days at Haviland Lake. I have a new fishing pole, and I caught four fish. Now we are at the Dolores River. I love it here. Tomorrow is my birthday.*

We drive to a campsite over on the Delores River. Don splashes the whole rig, including our truck and boat-topped trailer, through the enormous mud puddle that stretches across the entrance. It's mid-May, a little early to camp along this fork of the Dolores River, so the site is empty. We coveted this spot last summer, but other fishermen always beat us to it. We park in the conifers, where we have a view up the river. The children put up the pup tent for the first time in a month. Evening chill makes us huddle close to the crackling campfire. The air is crisp, and the aroma of pine smoke smells wonderful.

I go to bed wondering how we can make Amy's birthday special. We are camped alone. There are no friends to invite for a party, no grandparents to help celebrate, not even mail delivery. Gifts are few because we're traveling: a Good News Bible from Don, a small painting from me, and Nate has something up his sleeve. Pancakes for breakfast are the birthday girl's choice. I doze off as wind sighs through the pine trees.

---

2. With apologies to L. M. Montgomery's *Ann of Green Gables*, which Amy is reading. In the story, Ann finds poetry in everyday beauty; her highest praise is to declare that something holds "scope for the imagination." As Montgomery writes, "there was a passenger dropped off for you—a little girl. She's sitting out there on the shingles. I asked her to go into the ladies' waiting room, but she informed me gravely that she preferred to stay outside. 'There was more scope for imagination,' she said" (Montgomery, *Anne of Green Gables*, 10).

3. Einstein, *Hand of God*, 32.

"Hey!" Don is the first one up. "Come look at this!" Still sleepy, I crawl out of bed and peer out the window. Snow! *Snow!* We pull on clothes and burst from the trailer. The pup tent sags under a load of six inches of snow. We holler at the children to unzip the front flap of the tent.

"Happy birthday!" we shout. "Special delivery!"

What child from California doesn't think snow the best birthday gift of all? Exploration, snowball fights, snowmen—it's a great day. My cake experiment works: red and green food coloring and a few chocolate chips make the angel food into a watermelon cake. The little oven bakes beautifully. Amy is ecstatic, and to top it off, Nate's gift is that he will wash her dishes for ten days.

For ever since the world was created, people have seen the earth and sky. Through everything God made, they can clearly see his invisible qualities —his eternal power and divine nature. So they have no excuse for not knowing God.

—ROM 1:20, NLT

Old Farmhouse, Frederick Farm, Akron, Colorado

16

Colorado Prairie

Old Farm and Confession.

Farmyard reverie, art review, and glory gallery

Sketchbook in hand, I step out the trailer door and into the prairie morning. Fields unfurl in every direction—there's so much sky, I can see forever. I breathe in aromas of spring grass, dry hay, dusty road, growing wheat, moist earth, chickens, animals in the barn—all basic, down-to-earth, primal, life-nurturing smells. A meadowlark sings atop the windmill, which creaks and squeaks an uncertain treble *continuo*. Cattle bawl a raucous accompaniment from the field. Sights and sounds flood my senses. *Fill me up Lord, fill me up.*

We are snowed out of the mountains for now and have made our way back to the prairie farm to see Aunt Eva and Uncle John. What a beautiful spring morning. After that late snowfall, this springtime feels good. Aunt Eva has shooed me out of the farm kitchen, but Amy is showing her the "Hello Dolly" recipe given to her by our neighbor in the last RV park.

AMY: RECIPE FOR HELLO DOLLY TORTE

Mix ½ c. melted butter and 1½ c. graham cracker crumbs. Spread in cookie pan and press into pan. Over top, spread a 14-oz. can sweetened condensed milk. Then sprinkle 4 oz. flaked coconut over the pan, followed by 1 c. chopped pecans, and finish by scattering a 6-oz. package of semi-sweet chocolate pieces. Bake at 350 degrees for 20–30 min. Cool. Cut into squares.[1]

Nate followed Uncle John this morning, first to care for animals, then on to the fields. Like me, Don is on the loose with his camera slung around his neck. A mourning dove flies up in his face when he walks past a rusting disc machine in the side yard. We both edge closer. A flimsy twig nest with two eggs occupies the burnished metal seat. An anxious mama dove hovers in the cherry tree. We back off and wait. The dove returns to her nest. Don pulls out his telephoto lens to get close-up shots.

I sketch all morning—the weathered barn, the collection of rusty wheels in the dry grass. I have my eye on the grain storage bins, the dilapidated chicken house, and the old original farmhouse up the hill, now vacant. I have lots to sketch here.

> DON: *June. I explore boyhood haunts around the farmyard. I find another bird nest tucked into the corner of one of the windmill struts. Barn swallows fly in and out of the open hay mow on the second story of the barn. Chickens used to nest everywhere, but no more. Just a few of them wander about. Old haystacks decay where they stand. Makes for good mouse territory, which is no doubt what attracts the gopher snake lying in the grass. I scare up a pheasant that may have a nest in the hay. Over in the orchard, I spot flycatchers and warblers. They prefer the old fruit trees. Lots of bird life here.*

After lunch—they call it dinner—I settle into a yard chair under the weeping willow tree. Whispering branches fan away any hint of heat. Spring fever softens my very bones, and I drowse until Amy joins me. She sets up spelling homework on the picnic table even though we have declared that school is out. It's June.

I open my sketchbook and reflect on our travels, my sketches, and my observations. Am I evolving a style? Does my artwork have a certain look to it? Does my artwork have unifying elements? Any unique qualities? Is there hidden language or meaning beneath the subject matter? Does it reveal anything about me, the artist? I leaf through pages of ink and pencil sketches. Lots of analysis, but I doubt I can assess my own work. My drawings do remind me of others who sketch plants and animals, however.

1. We also found it in Seranne, *America Cooks*, 618.

Perhaps I'm a nature artist, at least in a limited sense. I can't yet settle down to one genre or one medium. Life is too interesting!

My reverie shifts to another subject: God's handiwork. Yes, I confess I am convinced it's God's doing. What triggered my change in thinking? When it comes to belief in God, I always thought you either have it or you don't. Instead, I found my belief grew slowly as I encountered the marvels of the natural world and explored the details of what holds it together. In my own limited way, I began to sense a wide scope of creativity, which is too vast to comprehend from any artist's or scientist's viewpoint, for it extends throughout the universe and beyond. Like an extended shift into drawing mode, suddenly I could see it: God has been there all this time. Belief is a different way to perceive the world, and it changes everything.

I'll don the cap of a backyard philosopher. As an amateur artist, the first evidences I have collected to affirm God's existence make up the components of *Order*. I didn't find unremitting chaos or even confusion, but *Order*. Nature's highly ordered structures, just like any successful work of art, exhibit these four major principles: rhythm, pattern, balance, and harmony. Harmony is the holistic concept formed as a result of interworking relationships that bring about a pleasing, workable, orderly whole. My artistic instincts find this a compelling formula for order. I can't stop there; orderly design is not the only thing I have observed.

Unity is an important part of the scheme of things. Living things contribute, influence, produce, consume, and relate to every other living thing. This unity results in a successful life community, whether large or small. Life supports life, and that means *Function* is important as well. Whether we have discovered it or not, each component of nature, as well as artwork, serves a particular function. This gives importance and meaning to its existence in the give-and-take of daily life.

The creativity observed in nature is apparent in its *Diversity*. The myriad varieties of forms, living and non-living, are astounding. The wealth of ingenious forms and exquisite detail suggests a Creator, not a random happening. Also significant is the enduring design—a mark of skill, artistry, precision, and caring. *Craftsmanship* comes to mind.

For me as an artist, the *Beauty* is undeniable. Whether it's in the small details or in their wide-ranging scope, natural phenomena trigger a sense of wondrous resplendence that feeds the soul. That admits into the discussion the *Spiritual* aspect. Depths of quiet solitudes and heart-stopping moments stir up the mystery of God that may unfold an all-pervading Presence, an extraordinary gift.

The grand scheme encourages investigation into what I sense as wholeness. Although I could not readily sense it in small slices of life, my understanding expanded as we explored a vast section of the West. I came to realize that these major art principles encompass not just art, but everything: rhythms of life, cycles of life, cycles of seasons, weather patterns, patterns of life, balance of life, etc. Ah, to be a farmyard art critic!

> DON: *Over by the road, the old windbreak my grandfather planted has matured. Chinese elms are a bit scraggly, never did too well, but the cottonwoods are havens for bird life. Wrens are nesting. I spot robins and mourning doves. The understory is a mass of brush. When I walk around, I scare up a pheasant or two. I look for the old badger hole I remember as a boy. It's been moved over a short way but still looks active. I also remember finding a porcupine in here, but there's no sign of it today. The original windbreak was three hundred feet by thirty feet. It has grown much wider over the years.*

I shoulder my art pack and wander up the hill toward the old deserted farmhouse. Windmill and water tank stand near the drooping fence that encloses the yard with its ragged shade trees and a weedy garden plot. The house is close to eighty years old, but weather-beaten walls stand as straight as ever. I place my stool in the shade of an old apple tree and sketch the scene. Don has told many tales of boyhood summers spent at this nearly self-sustaining farm. The old buildings tell their own stories. I can almost sense his grandfather striding across to the barn, with his grandmother on the porch shooing the chickens or working her vegetable garden, including her prized "wonder berries." Everything was done to make this homestead pay for itself—raising a variety of animals, using natural fertilizer, crop rotation, food storage, and growing animal feed. Nowadays, we would call it an organic farm. Back then, it was common sense and necessity.

Not much was purchased from town except farm implements, seed, clothing, and fuel for the coal stove. Gasoline was needed after motorized vehicles came on the scene. Discarded horse-drawn machinery litters the farm junkyard. Prairie life was a hard life and a lonely one, especially for the women, but what a legacy! The homestead life has been the backbone of America.

> DON: *I walk over to the quarter section that is still unplowed. This is short grass prairie. Grandfather used this plot for grazing cattle.*

Overgrazing has allowed prickly pear cactus to creep in. That doesn't seem to bother the prairie dog town. It's very active this morning. Grandfather realized prairie dogs were good for the soil and left them alone. Because of their holes and underground passageways, the rain soaks in better. Prairie dogs cultivate the soil by bringing deep soil up to the top. The colony moves its dog town every now and then. Grandfather noted that grass grew greener and higher where the old dog town lay.

I smell supper cooking. I sit on the back porch step and take a moment to jot down thoughts that have teased me all afternoon. If artwork reveals the artist, what does the creation reveal about the Creator? A theologian might list such characteristics as holy, loving, faithful, just, merciful, all-powerful, timeless, and good. As an artist, I add my own list of attributes that seems obvious from observing the great outdoors: Master Craftsman, God of order, creativity, diversity, function. Something nags at me; that list is not complete. What makes the creation "work?" The answer: relationships. Everything must work together—individual plants and animals, plant communities, ecosystems, even biospheres. Each part effects every other part. Harmony is built on good relationships. Our Creator God is revealed as relational.

The old pickup drives in from the field. Tired and hungry, Uncle John and Nate come trooping toward the farmhouse. They look pleased with the day.

I hurriedly scribble one more thought: when everything works in my painting, I say, "That looks right." When all living things function well, grow properly, thrive in their environment, contribute to it, and help sustain the system, we say, "It's right." Our Creator God is inherently good, being and doing what is right. The natural world reflects that attribute—it is good.

What's the Creator's style? I call it "abundant life" style. Who can match it?

I close my notebook and go inside to help put supper on the table. There's enough food to feed an army.

DON: *My afternoon is complete. I found a burrowing owl colony in one of the abandoned prairie dog sites. Even though they're mostly nocturnal, an owl stuck out his head to see what was going on as I set up the camera. I moved back a ways, and the owl came all the way out of his burrow to get a better view—so curious. Another came out and ran after a grasshopper and caught it. They're pretty fast runners, comical to watch. They summer here and then migrate to Mexico and Central America for the winter.*

How good it is to sit around the large kitchen table with our extended family. I savor the warmth and hospitality, enjoying the easy conversation as we laugh about old times over plenty of food. We linger over dessert: cherry pie along with "Hello Dollies." I'm so full I can hardly move.

Wind rattles the screen, and the light from the west windows turns a luminous coral. A crash of thunder draws us to the kitchen door. Fiery hues of red, orange, and purple blaze in the west. We exit *en masse* to watch the evening drama. An ominous and spreading dark thunder cloud hovers over the old house on the hill, and lightning strikes in the upland field. Wind whips trees, scatters leaves and road debris across the farmyard, and sends a spray of dust our way.

No thought now for art review, the storm cloud looms ever higher, larger, darker. A faint smell of moisture is in the air. Beyond the cloud, the vibrant sky still radiates color, form, and pageantry. The Master Painter is staging a brilliant moment in time, one that stirs the soul. The wind swirls around us and wraps us in an overwhelming cloud of memory. All the joys and sorrows, the lives and deaths, the loneliness and fear, the yearning and fulfillment of those who lived in that old house sweep through the yard. Days of yore, hopes and dreams, successes and failures have enriched the very soil, which is now made ready for new life.

Silenced, we watch the colors slowly fade. The tumult quiets as a winnowing wind blows dust across the prairie. Thunder growls once more, and we scatter back to the shelter of the porch. A few drops of rain cool the air.

"Come on," says Uncle John. "Let's go down to the cellar. The homemade rootbeer might be ready."

God saw all that he had made, and it was very good.

—GEN 1:31, NIV

View from Woods Lake, San Juan Mountains, Colorado

17

The Rocky Mountains, Colorado
Ouray Fourth, Fishing Camp, and Woods Lake

Fireworks, fishing, and focus—learning to see

July. Is this another perfectly timed "coincidence"? My last-minute call to the Ouray RV Park finds us the one available trailer spot left in town. We head to Ouray for the Fourth of July celebration. We will celebrate our year of freedom.

Truly in the heart of the Colorado Rockies, Ouray nestles in a forested basin. Mountains rise on every side, with the slopes a mix of conifers and aspen. At nearly 8000 feet in elevation, it is definitely breathtaking. Even though I have spent lots of time at high altitude this past year, when we walk over to the parade, I have to stop now and then to puff.

With flags flying and band marching, the parade begins. Floats and vehicles are festooned with red, white, and blue banners. Local musicians, dignitaries, and clowns roll past. We cheer them all. After the parade, the street is cleared for the children's games. Amy runs out to join the three-legged race. She climbs into a gunnysack with another girl, an instant friend. They stumble in about third place, puffing and laughing all the way. Firemen take over the street, and we edge out of range. They hose down each other's teams in a spirited and very wet competition. At the ice cream social, we savor generous servings. Ice cream is a treat, since we have no room for it in our trailer's tiny freezer.

In the evening, we drive up the town hill and join others who park on a secondary street. We chat with neighbors while we wait for the fireworks display against the cliffs. The evening is cool—a welcome change from our usual home celebration, where it is probably one hundred degrees. When it's dark enough, exploding fireworks light up the town in a spectacular show against rocky cliffs. At every burst, we "ooh" and "ahh" with the crowd. When the last spark sizzles out, huge stars in a velvet black sky hover over us as an aftershow of nature's nightly fireworks arranged in glittering display.

The next day, Don and the children decide to four-wheel into the high country. I beg off, wanting solitary time in camp; my excuse is laundry. They make a lunch and take off. About the time the laundry is finished and I'm settling down for a reading rest, they are back. I can't believe it. They burst into the trailer and announce that they took a vote. I must see Yankee Boy Basin.

Four-wheel driving is not my cup of tea. We barely fit the jeep road, and we meet more traffic than we'd like. As we approach a solid rock overhang, Don grabs the CB microphone. "Hello," he calls, "this is Old Hat. You got your ears on?" It takes two or three tries, but the fellow up ahead of us answers. Don continues, "I'm a four-wheeler, and we are close behind you. I saw you go around the corner under that overhang. How low is the clearance? We barely fit under this rock. Does it get lower?"

I stare out the window; no warning signs again. Backing out of this place would be no fun—it's a lengthy, bumpy ride along a cliff edge.

The voice answers: "No problem. It's lowest where you are right now. It goes up from there and you can make it."

"Great! Thanks," Don calls. We inch forward under the rock overhang; it's like a short tunnel with one side knocked out it. Around the corner, we stop and chat with the jeepster before we go on.

After squeezing past that tight spot, the basin opens. Wow! I am won over. Rushing streams cascade down mountainsides while lacy rivulets spread across rock outcroppings. Minerals color bare rock on the jagged cliffs that drop down to forested slopes. Knee-deep carpets of wildflowers cover the basin floor. Blue columbine are silver-dollar size. Indian paintbrush is so vivid that I'm not sure I have a tube of scarlet paint to match. We wander the area in wonder, overwhelmed by the beauty. The poetry of an old psalm seeps into my consciousness: *All the earth is praising your name. Alleluia.*

> DON: *Everyone votes to return to the San Miguel. We set up camp in the cottonwood grove. Just like old times, it's open camping along the river, and this is a clean camp. Room for badminton with plenty of downed wood for campfires. Nate's going fishing. After I clear the fire pit, I will too.*

This camping spot is like home away from home ever since we camped here last summer. Amy sticks around camp with me. The willows and cottonwoods near the water bend and nod hello in the summer breeze in what we take to be a personal welcome. As we wander about the meadow, I greet my old friends: first, the wildflowers—so familiar—Indian paintbrush, sticky geranium, wild radish, monkey flower; next, my favorite river rocks, those dependable subjects that held their positions until I got it right on paper; then the river riffles that taught me about flowing lines and still tease me with dancing foam patterns thrown like a fluttering scarf about the neck of each sizable boulder lodged in the current. I know other sensitive artists in the field also experience a certain bonding. I think of the early artists who came alone or on expeditions—Karl Bodmer, Thomas Moran, Albert Bierstadt, and others. They were so moved by what they saw that they returned home as advocates for preservation by publishing and displaying their works of the West. The spiritual aspects of their adventure were not lost on these artists either. Ruth Moran wrote of her father, Thomas Moran: "Every artist of genius experiences during his life a great spiritual revelation and upheaval. This revelation came to Thomas Moran as he journeyed on horseback through an almost unbelievable wilderness. To him it was all grandeur, beauty, color and light—nothing of man at all, but nature, virgin, unspoiled and lovely."[1]

When I start to draw each line and contour, render the important characteristics, place each marker, emphasize dramatic features, capture the textures—by the time I'm done, I feel like I know the very essence of my subject. The lines become part of my image vocabulary, while the contours and gestures stay with me. I close my eyes and can still sense the form of the mountain, the textured forest cover, the escarpments, even the snow patches. I will remember the peace that floods through me as I work, the peace that enfolds this whole community of life. I can sense it right here

1. Clark, *Thomas Moran*, 21.

and now as I set my stool in the shade and pull out my sketchbook. I love these mountains.

Amy reads in the camp chair while I sketch the meadow, the corral, and the trees beyond. We are serenaded by the afternoon breeze that rustles leaves and grass to the accompaniment of rippling water and an occasional birdsong. I grow aware of something else and look up from my work. Dust drifts down from the road; I see movement, then I chuckle. Hoofbeats are dampened by dust as a throng of wooly creatures streams along the roadway. Sheep. An entire flock. The sheep dogs turn the lead sheep into our meadow, and the whole lot of them follows. They pour down off the road in a fleecy, undulating mass. The dogs keep order with small barks as they circle the flock. Sheep scatter across the grass and into the open corral. A few wander over our way, grazing and baaing, but the dogs keep them away from our camp. It's a well-trained bunch.

> DON: *While I fish down river, I see sheep raising dust along the road. They fill our meadow—maybe two hundred or more. I reel in my line and go back to camp. Nate walks the log from the opposite riverbank. Across the road, a boy ties a couple of horses to trees. An old pickup follows the sheep. I walk over to talk to the sheepherder. Turns out he is the rancher who owns the sheep. He really warms up when I tell him I was born and raised in Cañon City.*
>
> *They have been driving sheep up here for years and are headed for the high country to summer graze. In years gone by, early ranchers overgrazed the high meadows. Now they are careful not to do that. "We keep them moving," is what he says. The sheepherder tells us he has just recovered from tick fever, which put him in the hospital for a few days. I ask if the sheep will keep us awake in the night, but they don't plan to stay overnight. Sure enough, in the evening they move the sheep about half a mile up the river to bed down.*

Next morning on our way to town, we drive past the sheepherder's wagon. It's parked just off the gravel road, a time-honored camp wagon design with a stovepipe. We wonder if the horses can pull it where a pickup can't go. We drive up the road to Dunton, an old ghost town at high elevation. As we climb the switchbacks, I look down onto a pristine meadow with a creek meandering through it. Meanders! At last, my final flow pattern. The stream snakes back and forth across a fairly level site in continuous S-shapes. Hurray! My list is complete.

> DON: *Drive the road to Dunton, which I saw as kid, but the old ranch community is now private property, and we have no access.*

Rocky Mountain scenery never fails, however. I find lots of wildflow-
ers to photograph. It's the greatest variety of flowers we have found
in one place.

When we return to camp, Uncle Jim and cousin Greg are setting up two small dome tents. Now the fun begins. All the men go fishing, but Amy and I walk down to the beaver dam. I want to sketch the active beaver lodge. Beaver have dammed several small rivulets that flow from the hill to form a pond right where they join the river. Away from the main channel, the surface of the cold, clear water swirls gently with patterns caused by the current. What a perfect example of my flow patterns! Plenty of contrast makes it easy to see the variety of curving lines. Observation and drawing have truly sharpened my eye. It's all about learning to see.

The neighborhood kingfisher streaks by and lands in a willow across the pond. He makes a racket with his piercing call. Amy pulls off her shoes and gingerly dips her feet in the cold water. Two muskrats paddle around on the other side of the pond and disappear into the grass on the bank. Perhaps they have a burrow over there.

Don appears with fishing pole in hand. He waves his fly line to dry the fly, then casts it out over the water. It plops down and floats on the surface as he reels it in. With a sweeping gesture, he casts again. A tree swallow swoops across the pond and catches the fly in midair. Needless to say, the bird is hooked. Don reels in the fluttering creature and gently releases the hook from its beak. It doesn't appear to be hurt and flies off. We marvel at its incredible accuracy and agility.

When we get back to camp, we find the fishermen are skunked—no bites, no fish. We rest on the riverbank and kibbitz. We catch up on family news and talk about the weather, but their minds are still on the poor fish-ing. The guys grumble; so far the only thing caught today was a bird. After hearing too much of this, Amy jumps up and announces she is going to try her luck. With pole in hand, she walks the log to the opposite bank. She throws her line in the river right across from where we are sitting. With a couple of casts, she hooks a good-sized trout. She holds it up triumphantly and marches back to camp—Amy the bold, grinning from ear to ear. The guys go get their fishing tackle.

Uncle Jim is not one to pass up a good swimming hole, so the next afternoon he and the children put on suits and head for the beaver pond. Access is idyllic, right off the grassy bank. The pond turns out to be two to four feet deep with a sandy-muddy bottom. The water is cold, probably from a snowfield. Amy stays close to the bank. The boys jump in, but when Nate comes up for air, his glasses are gone. The swimmers dive in the pond as best they can and search the dark water. We search the camp too, just in case, but we never find them. The next day, we drive to Telluride and call our home optometrist. Dr. Rob will mail new glasses to our next mail drop.

> DON: *I drive upriver to try my luck at fishing that stretch of water. Across the river are several beaver ponds that drain a marshy area not connected to the river. I wonder if they are ancient dredger ponds from old-time mining days. I'm slowly fishing past the pond area when—KA-WUNK—a beaver smacks his tail at me from the pond. For such a small animal, it's a surprisingly loud warning signal. I am not anywhere close to him, but his head pops up and he watches me. I wave my arms, and he smacks his tail again. I keep on fishing while he watches me. I catch a fish across from the main pond, and that brings another splashing smack from the beaver. He sticks his head up out of the water and watches me. I wave my arms again. He smacks that tail five or six times before I get out of range. I conclude he was disappointed that I was leaving.*

We long to get up to Woods Lake, and the next morning the men load the boat onto the camper. We put together a picnic lunch and take off. As we wind our way up the road, I see that Forest Service sign again: Beaver Park, two miles. The gravel road to the lake curves to the left, but I gaze to the right at the overgrown track that leads up the side of the mountain. Where does that go? What is Beaver Park?

This may be our last trip to the lake, since our vacation time is getting short. For once, the lake isn't crowded—just a few campers, including what appears to be hippies or street people over on the hill. Amy goes with Don and Jim in the first boatload of fishermen, and the boys fan out along the shoreline. I take my stool and backpack over to sketch the meadow and the trees. A day of solitude is just what I want. Drawing and painting are good excuses to sit by myself in a quiet area. Most people leave an artist alone, which suits me just fine, since I can't talk and draw at the same time. At any rate, the meadow calls to me; I'm sure the aspen whisper my name.

I stop by the old fence to look for elephant head flowers, but the bloom has come and gone. I find only a couple of drying stalks. The meadow is full of blooming grasses, black-eyed Susans, and an occasional scarlet Indian paintbrush. Blue-and-white columbine lurk under the aspen. I wander among the trees through the thick grass and sidestep the nodding columbine. I say hello to old flower friends still growing here, still robust with life, part of the thriving community. I climb up to the old ditch that runs full of water and walk along the trail for a ways. The variety of greens tickles my inner painting palette—how can anyone possibly do justice to it? I sketch for a while along the ditch bank. A current of images stirs my mind, awakening words of praise. Praise and prayer link to poetry. How else to express the overflowing senses? *Fill me up Lord, fill me up. I sing your praise. Your handiwork is wondrous. Alleluia.*

After a lunch break, I walk around one end of the lake. I sketch one of the mountain peaks that floats high above the forest. It must be 14,000 feet. The Pentel pen is fast and juicy, but sometimes I wish for a brush. Or both.

I wander up past the tent of the flower children and say hello to two girls lounging in their tie-dye dresses. I find an aspen tree that begs to be sketched. The stark white trunk rises from wrinkled, aging bark at the base of the trunk, where it turned black from storm or perhaps animal damage. This old-timer has its own identity. I focus on the lower trunk, so dramatic against the summer greens and wildflowers. Here is false lupine and sticky geranium. Each plant is so individual. Each has a distinctive design—similar of course to others in the family, but with its own unique characteristics: a scar here, a twisted branch there. Gerard Manley Hopkins called this "inscape."[2] The tree has its own reality. I use a pencil to outline the tree on paper. I try to render that reality, its presence and place.

In return, the old aspen speaks to me. Its very presence displays a life of meaningful function. Its contribution to the community, the finely crafted detail of its form, its life cycles, its circle of influence, reveals a lot. For me, it has become a witness to the Creator. I glance and sketch, glance and sketch, measuring the proportions against my pencil, checking the proportions on the paper, erasing and correcting the lines. As I work, I am overtaken by a deep love for this tree, the forest of aspen, these wildflowers, this hillside. Learning to see is how this journey began, and *seeing* is important. The truth, however, is that it's all about love.

A growl of thunder and a gust of wind make me look up. I hastily close my sketchbook against coming raindrops. I grab my pack and stool and head back to the truck. The fishing crew is already there. When they saw lightning on the ridges, they pulled the boat off the lake.

Sudden strong winds blow monumental cumulus towers our way, punctuated by lightning bolts from cloud to ground and tremendous blasts of thunder. The downpour starts abruptly, throwing a few hailstones at first,

2. Heuser, *Shaping Vision*, 25.

then finally enveloping us in a steady drizzle. The aroma of moist air and vegetation is intoxicatingly pure and sweet. I can't breathe deeply enough.

Before long, the drizzle eases, then stops. Clouds part and drift, leaving a rainbow that arches toward the misty mountain peaks. The pure high-altitude colors are momentarily suspended in luminous air before the vanishing mists reveal a second rainbow. Wrapped in the beauty of the moment, we watch the mists and colors change until, in perfect consonance, we hear silver tones of a flute as pure and sweet as rainbow colors. A gentle melody arches across the meadow from the tent of the flower children and enfolds us all, for shining moments, in wondrous community.

What a wildly wonderful world, God!
You made it all, with Wisdom at your side,
made earth overflow with your wonderful creations.

—Ps 104:24, THE MESSAGE

Aspen, San Juan Mountains, Colorado

18

The Rocky Mountains, Colorado
Beaver Park

Poetry, prayer, and praise

Today's the day. I have talked the crew into taking a four-wheel drive into unknown territory. Everyone is amazed that I am recommending such a road, but as always, Don is game. We look at the topo map and find the road comes out on the other side of somewhere, so we fix a picnic lunch and set off.

We cross the river and head up the canyon. It's a few miles to the fork in the road. The gravel road is scrabbly, bumpy, and as usual, muddy in a couple of places where small springs drain out of the roadside cliff. I cannot say precisely where I notice something different, but by the time we reach the signpost to Beaver Park and Don stops to lock the hubs into place, there is something in the air. A wayward breeze, the change of sun and shadow, and the summer foliage rustling a welcome—what is it? Is the earth off its orbit? Does the world turn more slowly? We leave the gravel road and follow tire tracks uphill into a cave of greenery. Unintentionally, my vision shifts into drawing mode, and all becomes poetry in the leafy light.

> *Jolting, bucking, bouncing up the four-wheel track*
> *We drive past aspen trees so close beside us on the hill*
> *I feel like I am walking through the woods*

Listening to a whispered conversation.
Above the road, the arch of greenery
Briefly opens up to sky and grassy knoll
Before we plunge again into the woods.
Climbing,
Slowly climbing,
The road winds through the summer's blooming grasses
And wildflowers strewn in carefree praise
Across the hidden ruts.
Where aspen woods thin out
The crest is smooth,
A sea of green now stretches out before us.
The high plateau, adrift with wildflowers and exuberant grasses,
Slopes downward to the farthest edges
Of the rolling parkland
Where, beyond the last etched line of forest
A solitary peak ascends in grand and lonely symmetry.
We walk into the meadow, calling all the flowers by name,
Exulting in the wonder of this place.
I breathe deeply of the freshening air,
Sighting birds and butterflies that flit across the blossoms,
Sipping nectar here, now there.
The wind picks up.
I watch it ripple down the slope
In rhythmic waves across the flowing plain.
Along the far horizon,
Storm clouds form and swell in towering billows,
Darker, darker,
Until a brooding veil of moisture
Wraps the lonely peak in mystery and torrent.
Whipping winds surge back to us across the parkland,
A rushing swirl and gust that halts us both mid-stride.
Expectancy and wonder
Sweep over land and sky.
The elements are speaking,
Humbling us in dust-to-dust remembrance.

Lord, do we intrude?
Is this a private drama?
The answer comes—
A hush, a fresh exhilaration,
And an overwhelming flood of blessing,
So palpable it hovers in the air.
This is why the Psalmist wrote of singing mountains,
Joyful hills,
And trees that clap their hands.
I sense the vibrant song of earth,
The sun, the moon, all shining stars
Aloft in countless numbers.
Small creatures, flying birds,
Wild animals, the cattle,
All join the parkland hymn of praise,
Jubilant with joy.
What beauty steals into my heart this day,
The Holy is at hand.
Our lunch becomes communion,
Tailgate table holding token bread and wine.
We sup with thee at Beaver Park, O Lord,
A wordless heart-to-heart repast,
Our spirits feasting on the stunning vista
Brought to being by your spoken Word.
Alleluia. Alleluia.

The sun swings past its zenith, and shadows linger in the grass. A hawk soars high on updrafts as its raucous call awakens me from reverie. It is time to go. We collect our scattered gear, load up, and head for camp. The ranch road leads across the open plain, but mentally I'm back up on the mountain, remembering the morning light, the wind, the mountain storm, the sea of grass, the flowers. Why such a time as this, why such a day? With God calling once again and the whole creation full of praise, I witnessed one more wondrous, joyous banquet for the soul. God's own cathedral is holding heaven on earth, and this day has sealed the lessons of my pilgrimage.

We pull into a central grove of massive cottonwoods that rise above the pastureland, where the windblown trees create a symphony of sound. The stock tank is full of water, but no cattle graze nearby. The road gets better past a ranch or two, before the track drops down to meet the paved state highway. Right on cue, my world speeds up. The earth shifts into orbit, and once again we drive the open road.

Shout for joy to the Lord, all the earth,
burst into jubilant song with music . . .
Let the sea resound, and everything in it,
the world, and all who live in it.
Let the rivers clap their hands,
let the mountains sing together for joy;
let them sing before the Lord.

—Ps 98: 4, 7–9, NIV

Juniper Bryce Canyon 8/14/77

Old Juniper, Bryce Canyon National Park, Utah

19

Canyon Country, Utah

Bryce Canyon National Park and the Last Sunset

Reflections, resolutions, and radical activity

DON: *August. First stop is Bryce Canyon Visitor Center so I can pho-tograph native plants by the building. Tourists start asking me about flowers. After awhile, the ranger leans out the window and says I should be getting paid. I guess I am slipping back into teaching mode. My pet peeve: study of biology that's all paperwork, not the real world. Nature is never boring. There is always something new to look at.*

We thought we saved the best for last, but after Beaver Park, that designation is arguable. Even so, I love Bryce Canyon. Amy and I linger at the viewing area on Yovimpa Point at the southernmost tip of the park. Today, visibility is good. We can see to the south for over one hundred miles, where the horizon line traces the North Rim of the Grand Canyon. They tell us a vast sequence of sedimentary rock layers stretches from Bryce to the Grand Canyon and down into its depths. It's much like a layer cake of nearly continuous geological history that spans over 600 million years. We stand on the top layer of the Grand Staircase—the Pink Cliffs. Below us are the Gray Cliffs, another formation. Farther out are the White Cliffs, and way out on the horizon we see a spot of red: the Vermilion Cliffs. The Chocolate Cliffs can't be seen from here. Each color denotes a separate rock formation from a different era. Forest covers most of the land over the ranges, ravines, and river drainages. What a view! A vast topography, geology in full color, and a thriving ecosystem—it's mindboggling.

Going home is bittersweet. I have bonded with the incredible landscapes in the American West, and here is another one. I could stay forever. The western states map in my head is no longer one of state lines and highway markings; it's been replaced by an extensive patchwork of ecological communities. I have begun to grasp what's really going on out here: plant communities are truly communities. Intricate networks hold them together in a web spun from plant to animal, animal to animal, animal to plant, and plant to plant. These close associations contribute to sustained life. Checks and balances hold these grand Earth systems in a dynamic equilibrium. I have learned my lessons well from the family naturalist.

I mull this over as we walk the Bristlecone Loop trail in search of Don. The footpath is shady in spots, but rigorous winters have pruned the vegetation in this windswept place. We round the bend and find Don photographing one of the oldest living things: a bent and scraggly bristlecone pine tree. It's a fairly nondescript tree, but I immediately scan the shape for drawing possibilities. Here is where artist and scientist connect. We start from the same point with ground-level observation. In our own way, we each want to bring order out of the chaos of a million details. No wonder Don and I find outdoor experiences our most enjoyable times together. It's fun to notice things many people ignore or have never learned to see. Don finds biological truth in behavior and relationships. I find artistic truth in creativity and beauty.

> DON: *Bryce has fine examples of living close to the elements: eroded limestone formations, tough species of plants that endure, and hardy animals. Getting lots of good photos.*

On the drive back to camp, we stop at every viewpoint. Technically, Bryce is not a canyon. It's the side of a plateau that has eroded into horseshoe-shaped amphitheaters filled with fantastic limestone sculptures, fins, and monuments. Carved over eons of time, the rock glows with earth colors like sunset skies captured in stone. Hoodoo shapes are the rounded rock lumps that appear to be piled roughly on top of one another. The wiggly column shapes are regular and irregular at the same time, a challenge to paint. In other places, fins of carved limestone project from the cliff like cathedral buttresses. The erosion cycle is still going on. Winter snows melt into the fractures, freeze, and thaw to cause more breaks. The summer rainy season is now upon us; every afternoon brings a thundershower. Runoff erodes surfaces and washes out cracks, and slot canyons may have flash floods. Like a school demonstration, the whole process is laid out before us. Don photographs. I paint a few quick study sketches and revel in all that rich earthy color.

> DON: *My dad said it: everything is connected. He fished and gardened all his life. I want to understand what's out here—the science, yes, but also the natural reverence that comes from being here.*

The wonders continue into the evening. After the program at the campfire circle, we follow the ranger to the rim for stargazing. We line up along the cliff trail. As if on cue, a shooting star as large as I've ever seen streaks across the horizon, right at eye level. Without skipping a beat, the ranger announces, "This opens our show for the night."

It's an astronomer's dream site. We stand in awe. Bryce is so far from city light pollution that the night sky is truly dark. A brilliant Milky Way splashes across the star-studded expanse. The ranger points out constellations and planets, making order for us out of the jumble of lights.

I gaze into the night sky as its midnight-blue depths deepen. Beauty and mystery surround us. The mystery resonates within me as once again my outward journey connects with my inward journey. The soul-stirring beauty of this night gives rise to a spiritual energy from my inner depths, reaching out to God, the Being behind nature. *Thanks and praise. Thanks and praise.*

I didn't come out here seeking religious renewal, yet the world of nature stirred up a natural reverence. I never expected spiritual encounters. Epiphanies were always a surprise. I performed no rituals, chanted no chants, did no deeds to attract the attention of a deity. Even so, the connection happened, and now I seek it whenever I'm out here. My view of the world has taken a major shift. It's all in the perception.

I resolve to follow up on my new spiritual awareness. After we get settled back at home, Don and I will look for a Christian fellowship. Why Christian? A year of outdoor life has made the natural world into a sacred pathway for me. The creation is a witness to the Creator God of the Bible. Jesus the Christ bridged the divide between the Creator and a struggling world, including the natural world. I want to know more about this God who comes unbidden, with soul-stirring beauty and a wonderful peace that reaches out to me so personally that I find myself responding.

At their truest, Christian values are life-giving. Love, forgiveness, sharing, equality, justice, and mercy are at the top of the list. Is that why life changed for the better after Jesus the Christ walked the earth? How does it work? That's another mystery. I want to know the whole story.

DON: *Nate and I took a side trip down toward the Paria River. We rescued a couple stuck at the bottom of a hill with their pickup and travel trailer—no traction for that steep grade. After a bit of maneuvering, I used four-wheel drive to pull them up the graveled hill. They were pretty happy. I knew they could make it the rest of the way. Glad to help out. We are all in this together.*

Wherever Don stops to photograph plants, I pull out my stool and sketch a while. The children scatter. Nate has the bug net out. He and Amy look for lizards, butterflies, and anything else of interest. We find aspen woods aflutter in the breeze, as well as wild edible plants for Don's book list. A red-tailed hawk soars high above the meadow. Along the rim trail, violet-green swallows swoop through the air to catch insects. The birds sport sleek, metallic green backs that end in purple at the base in a strong contrast to the white at their necks and underbellies. These handsome western birds probably have a nest in a nearby tree. A joy to watch, they dart into the grove with their insect catch. Is it my imagination, or does everything have a shine on it today? I pull out my watercolor pan and brushes.

Time and space stand still while I immerse myself in the color mixing before picking up just the right amount of water in the brush. I savor the flowing freedom of the brushstroke, feel the moment of impact on the blank page, then assess the effect, which can hold surprises. That's the challenge. I take a long look at my subject and try again.

For me, the act of painting has always satisfied something deep inside to fulfill my inner artist, but now there is more. Now painting is a means to an end, an excuse to visit the outdoor world, and an activity that holds me there. The spiritual values of being outdoors include the silence, the beauty, rest, recreation, and renewal. I find being outdoors a necessary grounding for daily life.

DON: *Lots of museum info on uses and domestication of wild edible plants. Herbarium specimen labels tell us where to find the plants in the park. It's rounding out my study.*

I can see firsthand how nature overall is a highly organized system functioning as a whole in life communities. If some animal, plant, or even an entire habitat ceases to adapt, it just disappears. If life events like this are merely mechanical, then the world is indeed

the sum of its parts. But nature study reveals more than mechanics.
This abundant life is greater than the sum of its parts. That's biology.[1]

One afternoon, the crew drops me off near the park lodge to draw an old juniper. I can't resist the gesture of barren limbs blackened by time and weather and topped with ragged clumps of foliage. I sit in the shade of a ponderosa pine and work with softer pencils to record the strong, dark contrasts of shade against light. Drawing brings such peace with its shift into a different realm of thinking: rendering images, making metaphors, finding symbols that hold meaning. Drawing and painting are a way to say, "Stop a moment. Look at this particular juniper or sunset or wildflower. Reflect on its qualities. Affirm its reality. Cherish it."

Have I learned to paint? I doubt anyone ever really masters watercolor painting, but a year of steady practice has improved my technique; sketching helps the brushwork. I have accumulated a stack of pen, ink, and brush sketches as well as color studies. Many of my paintings are now frame-worthy. I've made a lot of progress. I see so much more than I ever did before: sky colors that used to go unnoticed, tints and shades as yet unnamed, definitive lines and textures, the importance of shapes and contours, the edges of things, how parts connect, and small details that make the difference.

"Seeing is a radical activity," according to Michael Maynes. Radical because "*seeing* affects everything. Wonder and compassion go hand in hand."[2] Learning to see takes a curious mind, open eyes, open ears, and attentiveness, and I believe that anyone can do it. *Seeing* will change your life, your perspective. It is changing mine.

I love this grand outdoor world. I am resolved to join with others to protect this beautiful creation. I want stewardship of God's handiwork to be central to our way of life.

> DON: *My photography skills are vastly improved. I try to capture images that show relationships. I can use those in my teaching. But I'm not ready to go home yet—too much left to experience, to see, to learn. Of course, some things I can't do out here. The six hundred-year-old Aztec beans I was given in New Mexico, I need the greenhouse for that. It's highly unlikely any will germinate, but perhaps I'll get lucky.*[3]

1. Drucker, "From Analysis to Perception," 343–46.

2. Maynes, *This Sunrise of Wonder*, 235.

3. Out of 250 beans, about ten germinated and five survived. Don showcased them at his project review. Nowadays, we find Aztec beans for sale in gift shops and specialty stores.

The late afternoon sun dips in the west. Don and Nate build a small campfire for our last night in camp. At 8000 feet elevation, it's a bit chilly. Tomorrow my pilgrimage ends, and we will journey home. An itinerant breeze scatters sparks; Nate grabs the camp shovel and scoops the burning logs closer together. We eat supper at the camp table, shooing away jays and a furry thief in the guise of a chipmunk. Amy brings out the last of the marshmallows to roast while I carry dishes to the trailer. When I return, the sky is aflame with color, and I reach for my sketchbook.

En plein air means working fast before the scene shifts, so I pull out the pastels to make color notes. A wide band of thunderclouds—Payne's gray and violet gray—sweeps along the western horizon. Above and below it, thinner clouds burn scarlet, shocking pink, and vibrant shades of orange. Lowest on the horizon are streaks of gold and silver so bright I can think of only one word to describe them, the old King James "glistering."[4]

No time to revel in all that color, I work rapidly to record the clouds framed by silhouettes of the distant mountain range and the ponderosa close by. Working with sunset colors is a joy, but I have a lot to learn about color and all the possible relationships. My painterly soul has to deal with the surrounding areas that are not all joy color. Maybe I'll sign up for another watercolor class this fall.

The sun vanishes in one last swath of dark, rich red, a sunset to go home on. I close my sketchbook. In the gathering dusk, two nighthawks swoop overhead crying, *pee-ik, pee-ik.* One dives earthward, then zooms high again with that distinctive deep and sudden *whirrr.* The sound resonates within me; I wish it would do that again. The soft hoot of an owl floats from the pine grove across the road. Night settles over camp, and the fire burns lower. A breeze stirs the tall ponderosa in a soothing velvety sigh that signals peace. Chatter dwindles to nothing. We listen to the night.

Listening is a radical activity. To listen is to hear.

---

4. Archaic form of "glistening." Luke 9:28–35: "He took Peter and John and James, and went up into a mountain to pray. And as he prayed, the fashion of his countenance was altered, and his raiment was white and *glistering* . . . And there came a voice out of the cloud, 'this is my beloved son. Hear him'" (KJV).

☙

But ask the animals, and they will teach you,
or the birds of the air, and they will tell you;
or speak to the earth, and it will teach you,
or let the fish of the sea inform you.
Which of all these does not know that the hand of the LORD has done this?
In his hand is the life of every creature
and the breath of all mankind.

—JOB 12:7–10, NIV

Colorado Blue Spruce
on San Miguel River
Aug. 1976

Colorado Blue Spruce, San Miguel River, Colorado

To view Sabbatical Paintings by Janice E. Kirk, visit www.janiceekirk.com

Conversations with the Author

1. When the trip started, what were your expectations?

Freedom! Exploring new territory! Getting off the school schedule, which we had been living all our lives, from student days to teaching. I expected time to draw and paint. I had some apprehensions about living so closely together. Would we get along? Would the trailer be too small? Would we get cabin fever at some point?

On the other hand, we were experienced campers, even the children, so I expected we would all enjoy the trip and love being outdoors.

2. What was your art background at the time?

I did not major in art, but I did pick up classes after college—four or five courses in drawing and painting, including oils, and a year of printmaking, which was wonderful. I did three hundred botanical drawings for *Wild Edible Plants of Western North America* (Naturegraph), which was published in 1970 and is still in print. I wanted to paint watercolors, but I didn't know what I was doing. A year of practice would make a big difference. Just like any serious artist, I needed to go off by myself and figure out how to do things my way: learn how to handle equipment, gain brush control, develop my personal choice on colors, evolve a style, experiment with media, and discover my favorite subject matter.

3. Were you using instruction books or just painting out of your head?

To start with, I left the books at home, but over the year's time I picked up several. I'm especially fond of the atmospheric effects show in J. M. W. Turner's watercolors, and I picked up two books of his watercolors to study. I think it was the Taos Bookstore where I found John Cage's *Color in Turner,* which gave me plenty of nineteenth-century color theory to chew on. A couple of books on *Sumi-e* brush painting led to a lot of experimentation.

4. Why did the family choose to travel the Southwest?

Our usual camping trips occurred in the summer, but Southwest deserts are too hot for summer getaways and too far from home for quicker trips. Don chose to do a field study in Colorado's San Juan Mountains in the fall. His other area was Sonoran Desert in the springtime, when we could get to Death Valley, California, then Arizona, and as far south as Organ Pipe, New Mexico, on the Mexican border.

5. How did the family dynamic evolve?

We included the children in everything. The kids helped get firewood, washed dishes, set up their own tent, and took care of their own duffles and any gear they used. They helped set up camp and take it down. We functioned as a family, just as we did at home. During the winter months when days were short and the weather might have kept us trailer-bound, we went home. The children went back to school for two to three months until the mountain pass was clear of snow and we could head for the low desert.

Sitting at our family fishing camp in the Rockies, a friend made the comment, "It's wonderful to see a family where the parents are so relaxed." We had really kicked back, we weren't fussed up all the time, and the pace was unhurried and informal.

6. Do you have any practical advice for camping or traveling with children?

Everyone needs to stay warm and dry, sleep comfortably at night, and have plenty to eat. So choose adequate bedding or bring sleeping bags, pads, and ground cover to shelter from weather.

Choose campsites that are child-friendly. That means no dangerous water, no cliffs, and sites away from roadway with places to play.

Check out available gear: We started with Army surplus gear, remember? Nowadays there is more for kids, such as child-sized tents, but don't buy more than you care to handle. Keep it simple. We always had a pickup truck where kids could play if it rained and bunks where they could nap.

As to clothing, what wears you out when camping is not what you might think. It's not the physical activity so much as exposure to the elements. Being out in the open air all the time weathering heat and cold and wind and rain requires adequate covering and common sense. You don't see cowboys riding around in short-sleeved shirts and cutoffs. They wear long-sleeved shirts even in the hottest summer, with a bandana to cover their noses and mouths from trail dust and heavy-duty pants or chaps, boots, and a hat. They cover up. They have to. We may start out with city clothes, but we change pretty fast to jeans and long sleeves, learning to always keep a hat, rain poncho, and warm coat on hand. You will too if you want to stay out any length of time.

Plan on a regular Laundromat stop.

As to traveling, please no TV or movies in the car. Encourage children to watch the scenery, play the Alphabet Game, look out for antelope or other animals, name the highest peaks, sing, do roadside geology, or tell the history of the area to imagine the old days. Don't bring a lot of toys. The kids will prefer playing with rocks, sticks, dirt, mud, water in the creek, cones, and going fishing.

Cook over the campfire when you can—meat, kabobs, vegetables and/ or fish in a wire holder, biscuit dough wound on a stick, etc. Fix food the children will eat without serving hotdogs for every meal. One standby is a homemade batch of cooked hamburger mix that can be thawed to combine with chili beans, made into Sloppy Joes, or served up as Joe's mix of burger meat and spinach or any of your favorites. Boil spaghetti backpacker-style with very little water, covered, then take it off the stove and let it sit until soft. We had S'Mores now and then, and maybe once a week we roasted marshmallows, but otherwise we enjoyed fruit for dessert. Have a steady supply of homemade GORP with raisins, dried cranberries or other dried fruit, and cashews, peanuts, almonds, or other nuts, along with a moderate supply of M&M's to spark it up.

Steer clear of foods that take a lot of water to prepare or a long time to cook. Water is precious and fuel is expensive—and they may not be readily available.

7. What advice would you give to people today who would take such a trip?

Choose a destination and plan to stay. Trying to visit "ten parks in ten days" is exhausting and frustrating for everyone. Don't hurry—there's no pressure, so take your time. Leave space in the plan for unexpected opportunities to explore. Try to meet everyone's interests. Think the best, not the worst. It keeps everyone cheerful.

Do your homework and prepare. It's much easier now with online resources. Google the places you want to go. You can work out your route, make reservations ahead of time (some parks fill up fast), and check things before departure.

If you are planning a lengthy trip, take a dry run if you can. We took our tent trailer to the coast, which was about 150 miles from home, and stayed a week during spring vacation. Would our tent trailer be adequate for the big trip? No, it would not. Steady rain made the canvas damp around the edges. We couldn't keep warm enough. Wind was a problem. We had to get a different trailer. Figure out what kind of rig will work for you, then figure out the equipment you will need.

Plan how each person will spend their time. Once you have hiked and taken a look at the creek, what do you plan to do? We fished, dug fossils, looked for geodes, chased lizards, caught insects and identified them, kept a bird list, sketched, painted, and played games that didn't require a lot of stuff. More active doings in camp included modified badminton, horse-shoes, and sawing up firewood, if permitted. Don photographed, looked for wild edible plants, and worked on school projects. I sketched, painted, and sewed small sections of a quilt.

Warning: Most of the places where we camped as open camping are no longer open. Those beautiful spots may now be picnic areas or day-use areas only. On the other hand, available campgrounds are much improved, since they're often monitored by camp hosts and serviced regularly. Re-member that campground sites generally accommodate vehicles up to twenty-five feet long. If your rig is longer than that, you need to be sure of what's available before you drive into a place that may not be easy to get out of. If your rig is too large, you are probably not camping. Keep it simple.

8. As you look back, what was the low-point of the trip? The high-point?

The very lowest point was when we had to go home. Just being there was the high-point.

We ended up having favorite areas. We loved the area around Tuc-son, especially the Arizona-Sonoran Desert Museum. That is a must for anybody, as well as the Boyce Thompson Arboretum, a state park right off the highway about thirty miles east of Phoenix. It's a wonderful natural-style botanical garden. Get there at 8:00 a.m. when they open, bring a water bottle and a hat, and follow the trail. It's pleasant in the early morning, even in summer.

Other favorites are the San Juan Mountains of Colorado, Telluride, Mesa Verde, and Great Basin National Park. Death Valley was fascinating. Even though we stayed there a month, there was still more to paint. We also loved the Northern Californian coast, where we started. Our abiding sense of place covers an enormous area of land.

9. If you could paint one scene again, what would you paint?

I really wished I could go back to Death Valley. We were already preparing to move on over the last few days we were there when we drove the Artist's Drive. We thought there would be a lot of traffic on that road, so we didn't go until the end of our stay, but it was gorgeous. No wonder they call it the Artist's Drive! Every earthly color you can imagine is in those hills. I didn't have a chance to go back. I made a few color notes, but I would still love to go back and paint a whole scene.

10. Are you still painting today?

The only time I paint today is when we are out on a picnic or a camping trip, and I have plenty of time. Nowadays our camping trips are curtailed due to age and physical disabilities, but when I do get a chance to get out, that's the first thing I want to do. I reach for my sketchbook and black pen. I sketch with ink, freely recording a scene, a tree, a flower—I just start in. If there is time, I pull out my travel watercolor set and watercolor tablet.

It's hard to focus on two expressive arts at a time. Now I spend my days writing.

11. The trip was forty years ago. Why are you writing this story now? Why is it relevant today?

It has taken years to realize the importance of that trip, but the ideas and lessons we gleaned are still relevant. They are timeless.

At present, it seems everyone is into environmental thinking, but back then . . . Not so much. Ecology was only in its beginning stages. On our unhurried discovery trip, we glimpsed the truth of the Earth's dynamic system, learning that everything works in dynamic equilibrium. We returned home with a comprehensive viewpoint—a vision, if you will, of how life on earth is put together. We identified with plant communities, now called eco-communities, because the plant community is the basis for life. Of course, a plant community does not work without animals, so everything is involved, including humans. This is an important pulling together of previous scientific study, which separated plants and animals into categories, species, and the like. Those methods are useful for study in their own areas, but the new approach encompasses the wholeness, the interrelationships, and the unity of the natural world.

Writing about the trip has helped me not only to put it into perspective, but also to share the story. I think other people can gain from our field experience. I hope our adventures will motivate others to reconnect with the outdoors, learn nature's ways, study individual plants and animals, consider the large life regions and organization of earth systems, and learn how wonderful they are! And how beautiful!

We arrived home as different people. We laugh and say it ruined us forever for the workaday world, and that's true, but it was time to return home. We stayed long enough—we went farther than most, and we explored deeply. The understanding we gained remains with us and has inspired our work and writing, which attests to the experience's immense value.

12. Were you looking for a spiritual experience when you started out?

No. I was not looking for anything of the sort, but it found me. In recent literature, I find mentions of "Seeking the Sublime," to borrow a phrase. Adventurers, high-risk sports enthusiasts, and nature-lovers of all kinds are discovering an extra dimension in their outdoor experience. Environmental literature, art shows, and articles in outdoor magazines occasionally mention the "otherness" of certain moments.

I was not seeking any Sublime, but nevertheless I was gradually brought back to faith as I discovered the awe-inspiring Order, Unity, Creativity, and Functioning Systems amid marvelous networks of nature. In addition, there was always "something more." Epiphanies found me in wondrous landscapes and, at times, in individual "inscapes"—those intricate works of leaf and stem, fruit and seed. An unbidden natural reverence accompanied those experiences. The overwhelming sense of mystery, peace that transcended understanding, and soul-stirring beauty were undeniable.

13. Can God be found in the outdoors?

That's a big question! My answer is yes. The outdoors brought me close to what I consider the Source of what's going on out there. It's my major "sacred pathway." I connected that blossoming awareness to Christianity for several reasons. First, because that was my background originally, and

I knew the way back. Second, Christianity is linked to a Creator God, and I wanted to explore that understanding. Third, Christianity affirms life-nurturing values, such as love, forgiveness, healing, peace, justice, mercy, and sharing. Fourth, Christian principles establish a moral compass, and fifth, the Christian Way provides direction for a meaningful life. Having been field-tested for two thousand years, Christianity has helped a great many people. How does it work? I wanted to know.

For someone without a Christian background, C. S. Lewis acknowledged the need for some kind of map or guide to connect outdoor experiences with Christian faith.[1] Ask someone who knows about the Creator God and Jesus, the Christ. Find a study group. Get out The Message Bible and start reading for yourself how ancient people made the connection. If organized religion puts you off, listen to what Jesus actually says in the Bible. That's the Way.

1. Lewis, "Theology," 32.

Map of Southwest States

Bibliography

Clark, Carol. *Thomas Moran: Watercolors of the American West*. Published for the Amon Carter Museum of Western Art. Austin, TX: University of Texas Press: 1980.

de Fontenelle, Bernard. *Lapham's Quarterly*. Accessed December 5, 2015. http://www.laphamsquarterly.org/quotes/264.

Drucker, Peter. "From Analysis to Perception." In *The Essential Drucker*, 343–46. New York: Harper, 2001.

Duignan, Brian. "Occam's Razor." In *Encyclopaedia Britannica Online*. https://www.britannica.com/topic/Occams-razor.

Einstein, Albert. In *The Hand of God: Thoughts and Images Reflecting the Spirit of the Universe*, edited by Michael Reagan, 32–37. Philadelphia: Templeton Foundation, 1999.

Gage, John. *Color in Turner*. New York: Praeger, 1969.

Gaunt, William. *Turner's Universe*. Woodbury, New York: Barron's Educational Series, 1976.

Heuser, Alan. *The Shaping Vision of Gerard Manley Hopkins*. London: Oxford University Press, 1958.

Hopkins, Gerard Manley. "God's Grandeur" and "The Starlight Night." In *Gerard Manley Hopkins: The Major Works*, edited by Catherine Phillips, 128. New York: Oxford University Press, 2009.

"J. M. W. Turner: Style." *Wikipedia*. Accessed December 5, 2016. https://en.wikipedia.org/wiki/J._M._W._Turner#Style.

Kaplan, Justin, ed. *Bartlett's Familiar Quotations*. 17th ed. New York: Little, Brown, 2002.

Lewis, C. S. "Theology." In *The Joyful Christian*, 32–35. New York: Simon & Schuster, 1977.

Louv, Richard. *Last Child in the Woods*. Chapel Hill, NC: Algonquin, 2006.

Montgomery, L. M. *Anne of Green Gables*. New York: Grosset & Dunlap, 1976.

Mays, Buddy. *Ancient Cities of the Southwest*. San Francisco: Chronicle: 1982.

Ruskin, John. *The Elements of Drawing*. New York: Watson-Guptill, 1991.

Selz, Jean. *Turner*. New York: Crown, 1975.

Seranne, Ann. *America Cooks: General Federation of Women's Clubs Cookbook*. New York: Putnam's Sons, 1967.

Recommended Reading

Backus, Harriet Fish. *Tomboy Bride*. Boulder, CO: Pruett, 1969.
A delightful memoir about life in Colorado's San Juan Mountains during the height of the mining days.

Bowers, Janice Emily. *The Mountains Next Door*. Tucson: University of Arizona Press, 1991.
A botanist studies plants in the Rincon Mountains outside Tucson, Arizona, in this book of desert lore.

Burns, Ken. *The National Parks: America's Best Idea*. New York: Knopf, 2010.
The story of the National Parks' history, beauty, and natural resources.

Cather, Willa. *Death Comes for the Archbishop*. New York: Random House Vintage, 1971.
The story of early Santa Fe, New Mexico, told through the life of the first archbishop, who arrived in 1851.

DeWaal, Esther. *Lost in Wonder: Rediscovering the Spiritual Art of Attentiveness*. Collegeville, MN: Liturgical, 2003.
Readings for a time apart.

Edwards, Betty. *Drawing on the Right Side of the Brain*. Los Angeles: Tarcher, 1989.
Learn to draw using the exercises in the book.

Graf, Mike. *Danger in the Narrows: Bryce and Zion National Parks*. Golden, CO: Fulcrum, 2006.
A family camping trip to Bryce and Zion turns into adventure. For kids 8–13. Other books in the Adventures with the Parkers series cover Glacier, Grand Canyon, Rocky Mountain, Great Smoky Mountains, Olympic, Yellowstone, and Yosemite National Parks. These adventures are like the real thing: the text is engaging, authentic, and informative.

Kirk, Donald R. *Wild Edible Plants of Western North America*. Color ed. Illustrated by Janice E. Kirk. Happy Camp, CA: Naturegraph, 1975.
A ready reference to put in your backpack when you take a hike.

Leslie, Clare Walker, and Charles E. Roth. *Keeping a Nature Journal: Discover a Whole New Way of Seeing the World Around You*. Pownal, Vermont: Story, 2000.
Tips and techniques for nature drawing.

Maynes, Michael. *This Sunrise of Wonder: Letters for the Journey*. London: Darton, Longman, & Todd, 2008.

Wake up and notice the world for the first time and sense its mystery in these letters to the grandchildren.

Muir, John. *The Mountains of California*. 1894. Reprint, New York: Doubleday, 1961.
The classic story of John Muir hiking in the Sierras.

Murphy, Pat. *By Nature's Design*. Photographs by William Neill. San Francisco: Chronicle, 1993.
Learn to see patterns in nature.

Murphy, Pat, and Paul Doherty. *The Color of Nature*. San Francisco: Chronicle, 1996.
An exploration of the mysteries and science of color in nature.

Tomlinson, Susan Leigh. *How to Keep a Naturalist's Notebook*. Mechanicsburg, PA: Stackpole, 2010.
Detailed instruction on basic drawing skills and field notes.

Twain, Mark. *Roughing It*. New York: Holt, Rinehart, & Winston, 1966.
Mark Twain's classic tale of his adventures in the West.